Selected Early Poems

Also by Charles Simic

Poetry

What the Grass Says (1967) ∗ *Somewhere among Us a Stone Is Taking Notes* (1969) ∗ *Dismantling the Silence* (1971) *White* (1972) ∗ *Return to a Place Lit by a Glass of Milk* (1974) *Biography and a Lament* (1976) ∗ *Charon's Cosmology* (1977) *They Forage at Night* (1980) ∗ *Classic Ballroom Dances* (1980) *Austerities* (1982) ∗ *Weather Forecast for Utopia and Vicinity: Poems, 1967–1982* (1983) ∗ *Selected Poems, 1963–1983* (1985) *Unending Blues: Poems* (1986) ∗ *The World Doesn't End* (1989) *Pyramids and Sphinxes* (1989) ∗ *The Book of Gods and Devils* (1990) ∗ *Selected Poems, 1963–1983, Revised and Expanded* (1990) ∗ *Hotel Insomnia* (1992) ∗ *A Wedding in Hell* (1994) *Frightening Toys* (1995) ∗ *Walking the Black Cat* (1996) *Looking for Trouble* (1997) ∗ *Jackstraws* (1999)

Prose

The Uncertain Certainty: Interviews, Essays, and Notes on Poetry (1985) ∗ *Wonderful Words, Silent Truth: Essays on Poetry and a Memoir* (1990) ∗ *Dimestore Alchemy: The Art of Joseph Cornell* (1992) ∗ *Unemployed Fortune-Teller* (1994) *Orphan Factory* (1998) ∗ *The Fly in the Soup* (1999)

CHARLES SIMIC

SELECTED EARLY POEMS

GEORGE BRAZILLER
NEW YORK

A selection of Charles Simic's poems from 1963 to 1983
was first published by George Braziller, Inc., in 1985
under the title *Selected Poems, 1963–1983*. A revised
and expanded edition of this title appeared in 1990.
Charles Simic: Selected Early Poems is a further
expansion and revision of the 1990 edition.

Refer to page 256 for a listing of the books in which
the poems included in this selection first appeared.

For information, please address the publisher:
George Braziller, Inc.
171 Madison Avenue
New York, NY 10016

Library of Congress Cataloging-in-Publication Data
    Simic, Charles, 1938–
        [Poems. Selections]
        Charles Simic : selected early poems /
    by Charles Simic. — 3rd ed.
        p.   cm.
    ISBN 0-8076-1456-4
    I. Title.
    PS3569.I4725A6   1999
    811'.54—dc21
                                99-34872
                                  CIP

Designed by Neko Buildings
Printed and bound in the United States of America
Third edition

Contents

Butcher Shop

Sometimes walking late at night
I stop before a closed butcher shop.
There is a single light in the store
Like the light in which the convict digs his tunnel.

An apron hangs on the hook:
The blood on it smeared into a map
Of the great continents of blood,
The great rivers and oceans of blood.

There are knives that glitter like altars
In a dark church
Where they bring the cripple and the imbecile
To be healed.

There is a wooden block where bones are broken,
Scraped clean—a river dried to its bed
Where I am fed,
Where deep in the night I hear a voice.

Cockroach

When I see a cockroach,
I don't grow violent like you.
I stop as if a friendly greeting
Had passed between us.

*

This roach is familiar to me.
We met here and there,
In the kitchen at midnight,
And now on my pillow.

*

I can see it has a couple
Of my black hairs
Sticking out of its head,
And who knows what else?

*

It carries false papers—
Don't ask me how I know.
False papers, yes,
With my greasy thumbprint.

Tapestry

It hangs from heaven to earth.
There are trees in it, cities, rivers,
small pigs and moons. In one corner
the snow falling over a charging cavalry,
in another women are planting rice.

You can also see:
a chicken carried off by a fox,
a naked couple on their wedding night,
a column of smoke,
an evil-eyed woman spitting into a pail of milk.

What is behind it?
—Space, plenty of empty space.

And who is talking now?
—A man asleep under his hat.

What happens when he wakes up?
—He'll go into a barbershop.
They'll shave his beard, nose, ears, and hair,
To make him look like everyone else.

Evening

The snail gives off stillness.
The weed is blessed.
At the end of a long day
The man finds joy, the water peace.

Let all be simple. Let all stand still
Without a final direction.
That which brings you into the world
To take you away at death
Is one and the same;
The shadow long and pointy
Is its church.

At night some understand what the grass says.
The grass knows a word or two.
It is not much. It repeats the same word
Again and again, but not too loudly . . .

The Inner Man

It isn't the body
That's a stranger.
It's someone else.

We poke the same
Ugly mug
At the world.
When I scratch,
He scratches too.

There are women
Who claim to have held him.
A dog follows me about.
It might be his.

If I'm quiet, he's quieter.
So I forget him.
Yet, as I bend down
To tie my shoelaces,
He's standing up.

We cast a single shadow.
Whose shadow?

I'd like to say:
"He was in the beginning
And he'll be in the end,"
But one can't be sure.

At night
As I sit
Shuffling the cards of our silence,
I say to him:

"Though you utter
Every one of my words,
You are a stranger.
It's time you spoke."

Pastoral

I came to a meadow
Where the silence was the sky
And the words
The many wildflowers.

I stretched in the grass
With a hand under my chin,
As if leaning over
An open dictionary.

I plucked the petals
And heard the faint notes
Of a song
My mother sang to me.

Jagnje malo, the words said—
But when I went
Looking for the lamb,
It was nowhere to be found.

Animals and Birds

They have a way of looking at us
Straight in the eye,
These trembling toads
That get caught after the rain.

And the horses, of course,
Interrupting their grazing
To raise a silent question
In our sudden presence.

I shut my eyes today—
And there they were!
The suckling pig
Who only a moment ago was running,

The rooster with one leg raised,
Watching my eyes for a sign
Whether to remain like that
Or to go off quietly on tiptoes.

Fear

Fear passes from man to man
Unknowing,
As one leaf passes its shudder
To another.

All at once the whole tree is trembling,
And there is no sign of the wind.

Marching

After I forgot about the horses
And when the fire turned into cool water flowing,
And the old woman took off her mourning to enter
   a coffin
At the end of a long life.

A horse stood like an apparition,
A dream of a drowned girl cast out by the sea.
Suddenly he turned his head, bugler turning his bugle
To face the moon shining like a newly laid egg.

Then I rose in my house among my sons,
I put on my old clothes and my muddy boots,
My clothes smelling of wolves and deep snow,
My boots that have trodden men's faces.

I remembered the swamps, grass taller than horses,
Fast rivers softer than haylofts,
Where I'll stumble into deep hollows, dark eyelids,
Until I am buried under human droppings.

Blood rose into my head shaking its little bells.
In the valley the glow died in the udder of the cow.

The trees ceased playing with their apples
And the wind brought the sound of men marching.

A dog went along the road in front of marching soldiers,
A man who was to be hanged went along the road,
His head was bent, his face was dark and twisted
As if death meant straining to empty one's bowels.

So close the doors and windows and do not look,
The stars will come into the autumn sky
Like boats looking for survivors at sea
But no son of yours will rise from the deep.

Chorus for One Voice

I'm going to lie down next to you.
It cannot grow colder than this hour.
Strange men are gathered again
Drinking and singing. A different young man
Sits in their midst dressed in a uniform.

We are well into the night. Black moon.
With candle and spoon they examine its mouth,
A man with a dead soul and dog-licked knuckles
Eats from a paper plate.

I'm going to lie down next to you
As if nothing has happened:
Boot, shoemaker's knife, woman,
Your point bearing to my heart's true north.

*

This is a tale with a kernel.
You'll have to use your own teeth to crack it.

If not tonight, well then ... tomorrow.
Who keeps a clear head,
Who doesn't take a nap ...

There isn't much choice anyway,
It's too late to get your money back.

All I can say at this point—
You won't have to kiss anyone's ass,
Nor will you have to sign anything.
It will all take place on the quiet
The way love is made.

*

A sound of wings doesn't mean there's a bird.
If you've eaten today, no reason to think you'll eat
    tomorrow.
People can also be processed into soap.
The trees rustle. There's not always someone to
    answer them.
Moon hound of the north you come barking, you
    come barking.
It's not only its own life that man's body has to endure.

*

WANTED: A needle swift enough
To sew this poem into a blanket.

Sleep

The heart beats its little red drum.
In my legs, stiff like crutches,
And my head like a packing crate
Feathers of seagulls fly.
I'm with all that drifts out to sea
Down the big river at night,

Past some huge city on fire
With smoke-shrouded streets,
The crashing staircases.
A room with broken windows,
A bed with a mosquito net
Where a small boy lies sleeping.

Things crumble in my hands
Like singed photographs
Of obscured faces and places—
I'm whatever random scrap
Happens to blow my way.

In the dark I won't see the snow fall.
I'll listen to the flakes
Come down into the sea
With a dying hiss.

Psalm

Old ones to the side.

If there's a tailor, let him sit
With his legs crossed.
My suit will arrive in a moment.

All priests into mouse holes.
All merchants into pigs. We'll cut their throats later.

To the beggars a yawn,
We'll see how they'll climb into it.

To the one who thinks, to the one between yes and no,
A pound of onions to peel.

To the mad ones crowns, if they still want them.
To the soldier a manual to turn into a flea.

No one is to touch the children
No one is to shovel out the dreamers.

2

I'm Joseph of the Joseph of the Joseph who rode on
    a donkey,
A windmill on the tongue humming with stars,
Columbus himself chained to a chair,
I'm anyone looking for a broom closet.

3

You must understand that I write this at night,
Their sleep surrounds me like an ocean.
Her name is Mary, the most mysterious of all.
She's a forest, standing at the beginning of time.
I'm someone lying within it. This light is our sperm.
The forest is old, older than sleep,
Older than this psalm I'm making up as I go.

Poem

Every morning I forget how it is.
I watch the smoke mount
In great strides above the city.
I belong to no one.

Then I remember my shoes,
How I have to put them on,
How bending over to tie them up
I will look into the earth.

Summer Morning

I love to stay in bed
All morning,
Covers thrown off, naked,
Eyes closed, listening.

Outside they are opening
Their primers
In the little school
Of the cornfield.

There's a smell of damp hay,
Of horses, laziness,
Summer sky and eternal life.

I know all the dark places
Where the sun hasn't reached yet,
Where the last cricket
Has just hushed; anthills
Where it sounds like it's raining;
Slumbering spiders spinning wedding dresses.

I pass over the farmhouses
Where the little mouths open to suck,
Barnyards where a man, naked to the waist,

Washes his face and shoulders with a hose,
Where the dishes begin to rattle in the kitchen.

The good tree with its voice
Of a mountain stream
Knows my steps.
It, too, hushes.

I stop and listen:
Somewhere close by
A stone cracks a knuckle,
Another rolls over in its sleep.

I hear a butterfly stirring
Inside a caterpillar,
I hear the dust talking
Of last night's storm.

Farther ahead, someone
Even more silent
Passes over the grass
Without bending it.

And all of a sudden!
In the midst of that quiet,
It seems possible
To live simply on this earth.

Dismantling the Silence

Take down its ears first,
Carefully, so they don't spill over.
With a sharp whistle slit its belly open.
If there are ashes in it, close your eyes
And blow them whichever way the wind is pointing.
If there's water, sleeping water,
Bring the root of a flower that hasn't drunk for a month.

When you reach the bones,
And you haven't got a dog with you,
And you haven't got a pine coffin
And a cart pulled by oxen to make them rattle,
Slip them quickly under your skin.
Next time you hunch your shoulders
You'll feel them pressing against your own.

It is now pitch-dark.
Slowly and with patience
Search for its heart. You will need
To crawl far into the empty heavens
To hear it beat.

Bestiary for the Fingers
of My Right Hand

1

Thumb, loose tooth of a horse.
Rooster to his hens.
Horn of a devil. Fat worm
They have attached to my flesh
At the time of my birth.
It takes four to hold him down,
Bend him in half, until the bone
Begins to whimper.

Cut him off. He can take care
Of himself. Take root in the earth,
Or go hunting with wolves.

2

The second points the way.
True way. The path crosses the earth,
The moon and some stars.
Watch, he points further.
He points to himself.

3

The middle one has backache.
Stiff, still unaccustomed to this life;

An old man at birth. It's about something
That he had and lost,
That he looks for within my hand,
The way a dog looks
For fleas
With a sharp tooth.

4

The fourth is a mystery.
Sometimes as my hand
Rests on the table
He jumps by himself
As though someone called his name.

After each bone, finger,
I come to him, troubled.

5

Something stirs in the fifth,
Something perpetually at the point
Of birth. Weak and submissive,
His touch is gentle.
It weighs a tear.
It takes the mote out of the eye.

Fork

This strange thing must have crept
Right out of hell.
It resembles a bird's foot
Worn around the cannibal's neck.

As you hold it in your hand,
As you stab with it into a piece of meat,
It is possible to imagine the rest of the bird:
Its head which like your fist
Is large, bald, beakless, and blind.

Spoon

An old spoon,
Chewed,
Licked clean,

Polished back
To its evil-eyed
Glow,

Eyeing you now
From the table,
Ready to scratch

Today's date
And your name
On the bare wall.

Knife

1

Father-confessor
Of the fat hen
On the red altar
Of its throat,

A tongue,
All alone,
Bringing the darkness of a mouth
Now lost.

A single shining eye
Of a madman—
If there's a tear in it,
Whom is it for?

2

It is a candle
It is also a track
Of crooked letters;
The knife's mysterious writings.

We go down
An inner staircase.

We walk under the earth.
The knife lights the way.

Through bones of animals,
Water, beard of a wild boar—
We go through stones, embers,
We are after a scent.

3

So much darkness
Everywhere.
We are in a bag
Slung
Over someone's shoulders.

You hear the sound
Of marching boots.
You hear the earth
Answering
With a hollow thud.

If it's a poem
You want,
Take a knife;

A star of solitude,
It will rise and set in your hand.

My Shoes

Shoes, secret face of my inner life:
Two gaping toothless mouths,
Two partly decomposed animal skins
Smelling of mice nests.

My brother and sister who died at birth
Continuing their existence in you,
Guiding my life
Toward their incomprehensible innocence.

What use are books to me
When in you it is possible to read
The Gospel of my life on earth
And still beyond, of things to come?

I want to proclaim the religion
I have devised for your perfect humility
And the strange church I am building
With you as the altar.

Ascetic and maternal, you endure:
Kin to oxen, to Saints, to condemned men,
With your mute patience, forming
The only true likeness of myself.

Ax

Whoever swings an ax
Knows the body of man
Will again be covered with fur.
The stench of blood and swamp water
Will return to its old resting place.
They'll spend their winters
Sleeping like the bears.
The skin on the breasts of their women
Will grow coarse. He who cannot
Grow teeth, will not survive.
He who cannot howl
Will not find his pack . . .

These dark prophecies were gathered,
Unknown to myself, by my body
Which understands historical probabilities,
Lacking itself, in its essence, a future.

Stone

Go inside a stone
That would be my way.
Let somebody else become a dove
Or gnash with a tiger's tooth.
I am happy to be a stone.

From the outside the stone is a riddle:
No one knows how to answer it.
Yet within, it must be cool and quiet
Even though a cow steps on it full weight,
Even though a child throws it in a river;
The stone sinks, slow, unperturbed
To the river bottom
Where the fishes come to knock on it
And listen.

I have seen sparks fly out
When two stones are rubbed,
So perhaps it is not dark inside after all;
Perhaps there is a moon shining
From somewhere, as though behind a hill—
Just enough light to make out
The strange writings, the star charts
On the inner walls.

Poem without a Title

I say to the lead,
"Why did you let yourself
Be cast into a bullet?
Have you forgotten the alchemists?
Have you given up hope
Of turning into gold?"

Nobody answers.
Lead. Bullet.
With names like that
The sleep is deep and long.

Explorers

They arrive inside
The object at evening.
There's no one to greet them.

The lamps they carry
Cast their shadows
Back into their own minds.

They write in their journals:

The sky and the earth
Are of the same impenetrable color.
If there are rivers and lakes,
They must be under the ground.
Of the marvels we sought, no trace.
Of the strange new stars, nothing.
There's not even wind or dust,
So we must conclude that someone
Passed recently with a broom . . .

As they write, the new world
Gradually stitches
Its black thread into them.

Eventually nothing is left
Except a low whisper,
Which might belong
Either to one of them
Or to someone who came before.

It says: "I'm happy
We are finally all here . . .

Let's make this our home."

Concerning My Neighbors, the Hittites

Great are the Hittites.
Their ears have mice and mice have holes.
Their dogs bury themselves and leave the bones
To guard the house. A single weed holds all their storms
Until the spiderwebs spread over the heavens.
There are bits of straw in their lakes and rivers
Looking for drowned men. When a camel won't pass
Through the eye of one of their needles,
They tie a house to its tail. Great are the Hittites.
Their fathers are in cradles, their newborn make war.
To them lead floats, a leaf sinks. Their god is the size
Of a mustard seed so that he can be quickly eaten.

They also piss against the wind,
Pour water in a leaky bucket,
Strike two tears to make fire,
And have tongues with bones in them,
Bones of a wolf gnawed by lambs.

   *

They are also called mound builders,
They are called Asiatic horses
That will drink on the Rhine, they are called

My grandmother's fortune-telling, they are called
You can't take it to the grave with you.

It's that hum in your left ear,
A sigh coming from deep within you,
A dream in which you keep falling forever,
The hour in which you sit up in bed
As though someone has shouted your name.

No one knows why the Hittites exist,
Still, when two are whispering
One of them is listening.

Did they catch the falling knife?
They caught it like a fly with closed mouths.
Did they balance the last egg?
They struck the egg with a bone so it won't howl.
Did they wait for dead man's shoes?
The shoes went in at one ear and out the other.
Did they wipe the blood from their mousetraps?
They burnt the blood to warm themselves.
Are they cold with no pockets in their shrouds?
If the sky falls, they shall have clouds for supper.

What do they have for us
To put in our pipes and smoke?
They have the braid of a beautiful girl
That drew a team of cattle

And the engraving of him who slept
With dogs and rose with fleas
Searching for its trace in the sky.

*

And so there are fewer and fewer of them now.
Who wrote their name on paper
And burnt the paper? Who put snake bones
In their pillows? Who threw nail parings
In their soup? Who made them walk
Under the ladder? Who stuck pins
In their snapshots?

The wart of warts and his brother evil eye.
Bone-lazy and her sister rabbit's-foot.
Cross-your-fingers and their father dog star.
Knock-on-wood and his mother hellfire.

Because the tail can't wag the cow.
Because the woods can't fly to the dove.
Because the stones haven't said their last word.
Because dunghills rise and empires fall.

*

They are leaving behind
All the silver spoons
Found inside their throats at birth,
A hand they bit because it fed them,

Two rats from a ship that is still sinking,
A collection of various split hairs,
The leaf they turned over too late.

*

All that salt cast over the shoulder,
All that bloody meat traveling under the saddles of
    nomads . . .

Here comes a forest in wolf's clothing,
The wise hen bows to the umbrella.

When the bloodshot evening meets the bloodshot night,
They tell each other bloodshot tales.

That bare branch over them speaks louder than words.
The moon is worn threadbare.

I repeat: lean days don't come singly,
It takes all kinds to make the sun rise.

The night is each man's castle.
Don't let the castle out of the bag.

Wind in the valley, wind in the high hills,
Practice will make this body fit this bed.

*

May all roads lead
Out of a sow's ear
To what's worth
Two in the bush.

Invention of Nothing

I didn't notice
while I wrote here
that nothing remains of the world
except my table and chair.

And so I said:
(for the hell of it, to abuse patience)
Is this the tavern
without a glass, wine, or waiter
where I'm the long-awaited drunk?

The color of nothing is blue.
I strike it with my left hand and the hand disappears.
Why am I so quiet then
and so happy?

I climb on the table
(the chair is gone already)
I sing through the throat
of an empty beer bottle.

errata

Where it says snow
read teeth marks of a virgin
Where it says knife read
you passed through my bones
like a police whistle
Where it says table read horse
Where it says horse read my migrant's bundle
Apples are to remain apples
Each time a hat appears
think of Isaac Newton
reading the Old Testament
Remove all periods
They are scars made by words
I couldn't bring myself to say
Put a finger over each sunrise
it will blind you otherwise
That damn ant is still stirring
Will there be time left to list
all errors to replace
all hands guns owls plates
all cigars ponds woods and reach
that beer bottle my greatest mistake
the word I allowed to be written
when I should have shouted
her name

The Bird

A bird calls me
From a tall tree
In my dream,

Calls me from the pink twig of daylight,
From the long shadow
That inches each night closer to my heart,
Calls me from the edge of the world.

I give her my dream.
She dyes it red.
I give her my breath.
She turns it into rustling leaves.

She calls me from the highest cloud.
Her chirp
Like a match flickering
In a new grave.

*

Bird, shaped
Like the insides
Of a yawning mouth.

At daybreak,
When the sky turns clear and lucent
Like the water in which
They baptized a small child,
I climbed toward you.

The earth grew smaller underneath.
The howling emptiness
Chilled my feet,
And then my heart.

*

Later, I dozed off
In the woods,
Nestled in a small clearing
With the mist for a lover,

And dreamt I had
The stern eye
Of that bird
Watching me sleep.

Elementary Cosmogony

How to the invisible
I hired myself to learn
Whatever trade it might
Consent to teach me.

How the invisible
Came out for a walk
On a certain evening
Casting the shadow of a man.

How I followed behind
Dragging my body
Which is my toolbox,
Which is my music box,

For a long apprenticeship
That has as its last
And seventh rule:
The submission to chance.

Two Riddles

Hangs by a thread—
Whatever it is. Stripped naked.
Shivering. Human. Mortal.
On a thread finer than starlight.

By a power of a feeling,
Hangs, impossible, unthinkable,
Between the earth and the sky.
I, it says. I. I.

And how it boasts,
That everything that is to be known
About the wind
Is being revealed to it as it hangs.

*

It goes without saying . . .
What does? No one knows.
Goes mysterious, ah funereal,
Goes for the hell of it.

If it has an opinion,
It keeps it to itself.

If it brings tidings,
It plays dumb, plays dead.

No use trying to pin it down.
It's elusive, of a retiring habit,
In a hurry of course, scurrying—
A blink of an eye and it's gone.

All that's known about it,
Is that it goes goes
Without saying.

Brooms

for Tomaz, Susan, and George

1

Only brooms
Know the devil
Still exists,

That the snow grows whiter
After a crow has flown over it,
That a dark dusty corner
Is the place of dreamers and children,

That a broom is also a tree
In the orchard of the poor,
That a hanging roach there
Is a mute dove.

2

Brooms appear in dream books
As omens of approaching death.
This is their secret life.
In public, they act like flat-chested old maids
Preaching temperance.

They are sworn enemies of lyric poetry.
In prison they accompany the jailer,

Enter cells to hear confessions.
Their short end comes down
When you least expect it.

Left alone behind a door
Of a condemned tenement,
They mutter to no one in particular,
Words like *virgin wind moon-eclipse*,
And that most sacred of all names:
Hieronymus Bosch.

3

In this and in no other manner
Was the first ancestral broom made:
Namely, they plucked all the arrows
From the bent back of Saint Sebastian.
They tied them with the rope
On which Judas hung himself.
Stuck in the stilt
On which Copernicus
Touched the morning star . . .

Then the broom was ready
To leave the monastery.
The dust welcomed it—
That great pornographer

Immediately wanted to
Look under its skirt.

4

The secret teaching of brooms
Excludes optimism, the consolation
Of laziness, the astonishing wonders
Of a glass of aged moonshine.

It says: the bones end up under the table.
Bread crumbs have a mind of their own.
The milk is you-know-who's semen.
The mice have the last squeal.

As for the famous business
Of levitation, I suggest remembering:
There is only one God
And his prophet is Muhammed.

5

And then finally there's your grandmother
Sweeping the dust of the nineteenth century
Into the twentieth, and your grandfather plucking
A straw out of the broom to pick his teeth.

Long winter nights.
Dawns a thousand years deep.
Kitchen windows like heads
Bandaged for toothache.

The broom beyond them sweeping,
Tucking the lucent grains of dust
Into neat pyramids,
That have tombs in them,

Already sacked by robbers,
Once, long ago.

Watermelons

Green Buddhas
On the fruit stand.
We eat the smile
And spit out the teeth.

Watch Repair

A small wheel
Incandescent,
Shivering like
A pinned butterfly.

Hands thrown up
In all directions:
The crossroads
One arrives at
In a nightmare.

Higher than that
Number 12 presides
Like a beekeeper
Over the swarming honeycomb
Of the open watch.

Other wheels
That could fit
Inside a raindrop.

Tools
That must be splinters
Of arctic starlight.

Tiny golden mills
Grinding invisible
Coffee beans.

When the coffee's boiling
Cautiously,
So it doesn't burn us,
We raise it
To the lips
Of the nearest
Ear.

Traveling

I turn myself into a sack.
An old ragpicker
Takes me out at dawn.
We go shuffling, we go stooped.

Here he says is the blue tie,
A man climbed it as it hung from his neck.
He's up there sobbing now
For he doesn't know how to come down.

But I say nothing, what can a sack say?

Here he says is the overcoat.
His name is Ahab, his tatters are our tatters.
He is searching for the tailor who made him.
He wants all his black threads ripped out.

But I say nothing, what can a sack say?

Here he says are the boots,
As they sunk, as they went under
They saw their lives in a flash,
They'll cling to us wherever we go.

But I say nothing, what can a sack
Stuffed to its throat say?

Needle

At ghost hour,
Let one of your fingers
Walk the floor
Of this old house,

As if it were a
Dark forest,
With your dead mother's
Silver needle

In a bird's nest,
One lone drop of blood
Sliding down
To its sleepless eye.

Ballad

What's that approaching like dusk like poverty
A little girl picking flowers in a forest
The migrants' campfire of her long hair
Harm's way she comes and the smile's roundabout way

In another life in another life
Aunt rain sewing orphan's buttons to each pebble
Solitude's dark stitch
Let your horns out devil stone

Screendoor screeching in the wind
Mother-hobble-gobble baking apples
Wooden spoon dancing—ah the idyllic life of
    wooden spoons
I need a feast table to spread my memories on

Lone little girl fishing using me as bait
Me a gloomy woodcutter in the forest of words
I'm going to say one thing and mean another
I'll tuck you in a matchbox like a hornet

In that other life in that other life
Dandelion and red poppy grow in my backyard
Shoes in the rain bark at the milkman
Little girl playing blindman's bluff

The words are playing too—
You are *it* she says laughing and is gone
Divination by the sound of one's own heartbeat
Draw near to what doesn't say yes or no

And she had nothing under her dress
Star like an eye the fighting cocks have overlooked
Tune up your fingers and whistle
On forest path she hides herself behind a tree

I walk the way you vanished spellbound
Not even the wind blew to remind me of time
Approaches that which they insist on calling happiness
The nightbird says its name

On your arms raised high hoist this vision
Some evening when they come to quiz you in love
Glancing back under the dark trees
Little girl skipping the owls' hushed way

Solving the Riddle

The shadow is a clue. O shadow!
I carry my clues in a sieve.

Whose clues?
All my fibbing, double-crossing clues,
It's time we solve the riddle.

Mr. Clue says nothing.
The white dog he sent out
On an errand
Hasn't come back yet.

*

I look at the lines in my hand.
They form a maze
It's easy to get lost in.
No one to ask for directions,

So I ask my ears,
My ears full of whispers.
So I ask my eyes,

My eyes still not sure
Whether they see better
Open or shut.

*

It goes roundabout
And roundabout
Changing its guises.
What do you care? I said to myself.

I've set a trap for it
With myself as bait.
Motes of dust touched with gold
Twirled in the dying sunlight.

Shadows on the wall.
Made their faces,
Thumbed their noses,
And that was all.

*

Like the clock
On the wall,

One minute
It's nothing,
The next minute
It's something

Something thinking
About nothing
And making
A solitary tick.

*

In a riddle,
Which keeps changing
Its answer,
I sat myself down to pray.

The night was a meadow.
Black sheep grazing
Around a white gravestone,
The shepherd in a long cape

Up there among them . . .
I only heard its rustle.
And it was like the sound of leaves
Waking in a cypress grove.

The Place

They were talking about the war,
The table still uncleared in front of them.
Across the way, the first window
Of the evening was already lit.
He sat, hunched over, quiet,
The old fear coming over him . . .
It grew darker. She got up to take the plate—
Now unpleasantly white—to the kitchen.
Outside in the fields, in the woods,
A bird spoke in proverbs,
A Pope went out to meet Attila,
The ditch was ready for its squad.

Breasts

I love breasts, hard
Full breasts, guarded
By a button.

They come in the night.
The bestiaries of the ancients
Which include the unicorn
Have kept them out.

Pearly, like the east
An hour before sunrise,
Two ovens of the only
Philosopher's stone
Worth bothering about.

They bring on their nipples
Beads of inaudible sighs,
Vowels of delicious clarity
For the little red schoolhouse of our mouths.

Elsewhere, solitude
Makes another gloomy entry
In its ledger, misery
Borrows another cup of rice.

They draw nearer: Animal
Presence. In the barn
The milk shivers in the pail.

I like to come up to them
From underneath, like a kid
Who climbs on a chair
To reach a jar of forbidden jam.

Gently, with my lips,
Loosen the button.
Have them slip into my hands
Like two freshly poured beer mugs.

I spit on fools who fail to include
Breasts in their metaphysics,
Stargazers who have not enumerated them
Among the moons of the earth . . .

They give each finger
Its true shape, its joy:
Virgin soap, foam
On which our hands are cleansed.

And how the tongue honors
These two sour buns,
For the tongue is a feather
Dipped in egg yolk.

I insist that a girl
Stripped to the waist
Is the first and last miracle,
That the old janitor on his deathbed
Who demands to see the breasts of his wife
For one last time
Is the greatest poet who ever lived.

O my sweet yes, my sweet no,
Look, everyone is asleep on the earth.
Now, in the absolute immobility
Of time, drawing the waist
Of the one I love to mine,

I will tip each breast
Like a dark heavy grape
Into the hive
Of my drowsy mouth.

Charles Simic

Charles Simic is a sentence.
A sentence has a beginning and an end.

Is he a simple or compound sentence?
It depends on the weather,
It depends on the stars above.

What is the subject of the sentence?
The subject is your beloved Charles Simic.

How many verbs are there in the sentence?
Eating, sleeping, and fucking are some of its verbs.

What is the object of the sentence?
The object, my little ones,
Is not yet in sight.

And who is writing this awkward sentence?
A blackmailer, a girl in love,
And an applicant for a job.

Will they end with a period or a question mark?
They'll end with an exclamation point and an ink spot.

Closed House

Father, what are you doing
With that cane?
It skips ahead of you
Chattering to itself.

When a hump grew
On your back,
The cane's shadow
Came to keep
Your shadow company.

*

I remember your story
About following footprints
In the new snow,
That came to an abrupt end.

You were six years old.
Your mother had sent you at daybreak
To summon a midwife,
And you stood there puzzled.

*

You've been gone a long time,
Father, and now your mother,
Whom I never knew,
Has joined me here by the window.

She has a small accordion
Which she squeezes with her eyes closed.
Sometimes I think I can hear the tune.
Sometimes I think I can hear your cane tapping.

Solitude

There now, where the first crumb
Falls from the table
You think no one hears it
As it hits the floor,

But somewhere already
The ants are putting on
Their Quaker hats
And setting out to visit you.

The Point

This is the story
Afraid to go on.

This is the iron cradle
Of the stillness
That rocks the story
Afraid to go on.

How it regrets
The loss of its purity,
The madness of this
Single burnt consonant,

Which now sits,
Shy, solitary,
Among all these
White spaces.

*

And it dreams,
The story afraid to go on.

In its dream it builds itself
In the shape
Of the gallows tree.

When the gallows are completed,
It hangs by the neck
What's left of its dreamings.

Underneath, in the dirt,
The shadow of its beginning
Comes to nibble
Its quivering feet.

                *

There's no point,
Says the story
Afraid to go on.

It's all a question
Of the mote
In your eye.

It watches
As you watch.

Perhaps this evening
Reflects its final blackness,
Reflects its final mourning

Before it dissolves
Into a tear?

*

After its death,
They opened the story
Afraid to go on.
And found nothing.

Inside nothing,
They found a slip
Of the tongue.
Inside the tongue,
A loose hair.
Inside the hair,
They found

Whatever
Is destroyed
Each time
It is named.

The Pillow

Are we still traveling?
Whiteness, you came out of a dog's mouth
On a cold day. Apron,
I lie within you like an apple.

You've lit up my forest. Two
Black winds you sell. Do you still
Guard me from robbers
On the road fearsome and lonesome?

To tie my breath inside you
Into a knot—find the way
Back to your old scent—
It still hasn't brought me a mockingbird.

We separated, sacred time.
I stretch between two chairs. Recently
I started wearing blinders. One-legged,
Since there's no room for the other.

The dead love eggs. This is
That stone tucked beneath you
Speaking. Bared now,
For those who grit their teeth in sleep

To lay down their heads.

The Soup

Together in the pot
With our lives
Chopped like onions.

Let it rain, let it snow.
Dead people's wedding pictures
Make a hearty soup.

    *

The soup of strays
Roaming the world
In search of their master.

The soup of orphans
Wiping their red noses
On the black armband on their sleeves.

The soup loved by flies.

    *

On what shall we cook it?

On the mustache of Joseph Stalin.
The fires of Treblinka.

The fires of Hiroshima.
The head of the one about to be shot.
The head swarming with memories.

Let's cook it until we see in its steam
Our sweethearts' white bodies.
They are huge, they are voluptuous,
They are offering their breasts to us
As if we were suckling infants.

    *

What do you think it will taste like?

Like spit on a pair of dice.
Like prison barbed wire.
Like white panties of Veronica Lake.
Like her toes painted red.
Like tallow on death's wheelbarrow.

At the end of an evil century,
We arouse the devil's curiosity
By spooning the soup of angels
Into our toothless mouths.

    *

What shall we eat it with?

With an old shoe left in the rain.
With two eyes quarreling in the same head.
With a bent and rusty nail
And a trembling hand.

We'll sit slurping
With our hats on:
A soup like knives being sharpened.
A thick slaughterhouse soup.

*

And this is what we'll have on the side:

The bread of remembrance, a black bread.
Blood sausages of yes and no.
Scallions grown on our mothers' graves.
Black olives from our fathers' eyes.

The immigrant in the middle of the Atlantic,
Pissing in the sea with a sense of eternity.
The wine of that clear night,
A dark wine sparkling with stars.

The Chicken without a Head

1

When two times two was three,
The chicken without a head was hatched.
When the earth was still flat,
It fell off its edge, daydreaming.
When there were 13 signs in the zodiac,
It found a dead star for its gizzard.
When the first fox was getting married,
It taught itself to fly with one wing.
When all the eggs were still golden,
The clouds in the sky tasted like sweet corn.
When the rain flooded its coop,
Its wishbone was its ark.
Ah, when the chicken had only itself to roast,
The lightning was its skewer,
The thunder its baste and salt.

2

The chicken without a head made a sigh,
And then a hailstone out of that sigh,
And the window for the hailstone to strike.
Nine lives it made for itself,
And nine coats of solitude to dress them in.
It made its own shadow. No, I'm lying.

It only made a flea to bite some holes in the shadow.
Made it all out of nothing. Made a needle
To sew back its broken eggshell.
Made the lovers naked. Everybody else put clothes
  on them.
Its father made the knife, but it polished the blade,
Until it threw back its image like a funhouse mirror.
Made it all out of raglets of time.
Who's to say it'd be happier if it didn't?

3

Hear the song of a chicken without a head
As it goes scratching in grave dirt.
A song in which two parallel lines
Meet at infinity, in which God
Makes the last of the little apples,
In which golden fleece is heard growing
On a sad girl's pubes. The song
Of swearwords dreaming of a pure mouth.
The song of a doornail raised from the dead.
The song of circumspection because accomplices
Have been found, because the egg's safe
In the cuckoo's nest. The song
You wade into until your own hat floats.
A song of contagious laughter.
A lethal song.
That's right, the song of premonition.

4

On a headless evening of a headless day
The chicken on fire and the words
Around it like a ring of fabulous beasts.
Each night it threw them a bite-size portion of its
    heart.
The words were hungry, the night held the fork.
Whatever our stylish gallows bird made, its head
    unmade,
Its long-lost, axed-off sultan's head
Rose into the sky in a balloon of fiery numerals.
Down below the great feast went on:
The table that supplies itself with bread.
A saw that cuts a dream in half.
Wings so quick they don't get wet in heavy rain.
The egg that mutters to the frying pan:
I swear it by the hair in my yolk,
There's no such thing as a chicken without a head.

5

The chicken without a head ran a maze,
Ran half-plucked,
A serving fork stuck in its back,
Ran, backward, into the blue of the evening.
Ran upside down,
Its drumsticks and talons in the clouds.

Someone huge and red-aproned rose in its wake.
Many black umbrellas parting to let it pass.
Ran leaving its squinting head far behind,
Its head reeking of barber's cologne.
Ran up the church steeple,
Up the lightning rod on that steeple
For the wind to hone its prettiest plumes.
Ran, and is still running this Good Friday,
Between raindrops,
Hellfoxes on its trail.

White

Out of poverty
To begin again

With the taste of silence
On my tongue

Say a word,
Then listen to it fray

Thread by thread,
In the fading,

The already vanishing
Evening light.

    *

So clear, it's obscure
The sense of existing

In this very moment,
Cheek by jowl with

My shadow on the wall
With its long, gallowslike,

Contorted neck
Bloodied by the sunset,

Watching and listening
To my own heartbeat.

*

This is breath, only breath.
Think it over, friend.

A shit-house fly weighs
Twice as much.

But when I tell the world so,
I'm less by a breath.

The struck match flares up
And nods in agreement

Before the dark claps it
With its heavy hands.

*

As strange as a shepherd
In the Arctic Circle.

Someone like Bo-peep.
All her sheep are white

And she can't get any sleep
Over lost sheep,

And she's got a flute
Which cries Bo-peep,

Which says, poor girl,
Take care of your sheep.

*

On a late afternoon of snow,
In a small unlit grocery store

Where a door has just opened
With a long, painful squeak,

A small boy carries a piece of paper
Between his thumb and forefinger

To the squint-eyed old woman
Bending low over the counter.

It's that paper I'm remembering,
And the quiet and the shadows.

*

You're not what you seem to be.
I'm not what I seem to be.

It's as if we were the unknowing
Inmates of someone's shadow box,

And the curtain was our breath
And so were the stage sets

Which were like the world we know.
His gloves are as gray as the sky

While he holds us up by our feet
Swaying over the earth to and fro.

     *

We need a marrying preacher.
Some crow, praise be,

By the side of the road
With a sun-reddened beak

Studying a wind-leafed
Black book

All of whose pages are gold-edged
And blank,

As we wait, with frost thickening
On our eyelashes.

*

The sky of the desert,
The heavens of the crucified.

The great white sky
Of the visionaries.

Its one lone, ghostlike
Buzzard hovering,

Writing the long century's
Obituary column

Over the white city,
The city of our white nights.

*

Mother gives me to the morning
On the threshold.

I have the steam of my breath
For a bride.

The snow on my shoes
The hems of her wedding dress,

My love always a step ahead,
Always a blur,

A whiteout
In the raging, dreamlike storm.

    *

As if I shut my eyes
In order to peek

At the world unobserved,
And saw

The nameless
In its glory.

And knew no way
To speak of it,

And did, nevertheless,
And then said something else.

    *

What are you up to smart ass?
I turn on my tongue's skewer.

What do you baste yourself with?
I spit bile laced with blood.

Do you sprinkle pepper and salt?
I bite words as they come into my mouth.

And how will you know you're done?
My eyes will burn till I see clear.

What will you carve yourself with?
I'll let my tongue be the knife.

*

In the inky forest,
In its maziest,

Murkiest scribble
Of words

And wordless cries,
I went for a glimpse

Of the blossomlike
White erasure

Over a huge,
Furiously crossed-out something.

*

I can't say I'm much of a cook,
If my heart is in the fire with the onions.

I can't say I'm much of a hero,
If the weight of my head has me pinned down.

I can't say I'm the boss here,
If the flies hang their hats in my mouth.

I can't say I got the smarts,
If I wait for the evening star to answer me.

Nor can I call myself good-for-nothing.
Thanks to me the worms will have their feast.

    *

One has to make do.
Make ends meet,

Odds and ends.
Make no bones about it.

Make a stab in the dark.
Make the hair curl.

Make a door-to-nowhere.
Make a megaphone with one's hands,

And call and make do
With the silence answering.

    *

Then all's well and white
All day and all night.

The highways are snowbound.
The forest paths are hushed.

The power lines have fallen.
The windows are dark.

Nothing but starlight
And the snow's dim light

And the wind wildly
Preaching in the pine tree.

      *

In an unknown year
Of an all-evil century,

On a day of frost and biting wind,
A tiny old woman,

One foot in the grave,
Met a boy playing hooky.

She offered him a sugar cube
In a hand so wizened

His tongue twisted into a knot
Saying thanks.

*

Do you take this line
Stretching to infinity?

I take this white paper
Lying still before me.

Do you take this ring
That has no known circumference?

I take this breath
Slipping in and out of it.

Then you may kiss the dot
Where your pencil fell on its lead.

*

Had to get through me
On its long trek

To and from nowhere.
Woe to every heartbeat

That stood in its way,
Woe to every thought ...

Time's white ants,
The rustle of their feet.

Gravedigger ants.
Village idiot ants.

*

I haven't budged from the beginning.
Five fingers crumpled up

Over the blank page
Like a love letter,

Do you hear the white night
Touching down?

I hear the ear trumpets,
The holy escutcheons

Turning golden
In the dying light.

*

Psst. The white hair
Fallen from my head

On the writing paper
Momentarily unidentified.

I had to bend down low
And put my eye next to it

To make sure,
Then nudge it, ever so slowly

With the long tip of my pen
Over the edge of the table.

What the White Had to Say

Because I'm nothing you can name,
I knew you long before you knew me.
Some days you keep your hand closed
As if you've caught me,
But it's only a fly you've got there.
No use calling on angels and devils
In the middle of the night.
Go ahead, squint into the dregs on the bottom
Of your coffee cup, for all I care.
I do not answer to your hocus-pocus,
For I'm nearer to you than your own breath.
One sun shines on us both
Through the slit in your eyelids.
Your empty hand shows me off
To the four white walls of your room,
While with my horse's tail I wave the fly away,
But there's no tail, and the fly
Is a white thought buzzing in your head.

Because I'm nothing you'll ever name,
You sharpen your tongue hoping to skewer me.
The ear that rose in the night
To hear the truth inside the word *love*.
Listen to this, my beloved nothing,

I'm the great nothing that tucked you in,
The finger placed softly on your lips
That made you sit up in bed wide-awake.
Still, this riddle comes with no answer.
The same mother left us on your doorstep.
The same high ceiling made us insomniac.
Late-night piano picking out blue notes
In the empty ballroom down the hall,
We are in the hole between them.
And still you want me to say more?
Time has stopped. Your shadow,
With its gallowslike crooked neck
Listening to me, has not stirred on the wall.

The Partial Explanation

Seems like a long time
Since the waiter took my order.
Grimy little luncheonette,
The snow falling outside.

Seems like it has grown darker
Since I last heard the kitchen door
Behind my back
Since I last noticed
Anyone pass on the street.

A glass of ice water
Keeps me company
At this table I chose myself
Upon entering.

And a longing,
Incredible longing
To eavesdrop
On the conversation
Of cooks.

The Lesson

It occurs to me now
that all these years
I have been
the idiot pupil
of a practical joker.

Diligently
and with foolish reverence
I wrote down
what I took to be
his wise pronouncements
concerning
my life on earth.
Like a parrot
I rattled off the dates
of wars and revolutions.
I rejoiced
at the death of my tormentors.
I even became convinced
that their number
was diminishing.

It seemed to me
that gradually

my teacher was revealing to me
a pattern,
that what I was being told
was an intricate plot
of a picaresque novel
in installments,
the last pages of which
would be given over
entirely
to lyrical evocations
of nature.

Unfortunately,
with time,
I began to detect in myself
an inability
to forget even
the most trivial detail.
I lingered more and more
over the beginnings:
The haircut of a soldier
who was urinating
against our fence;
shadows of trees on the ceiling,
the day
my mother and I
had nothing to eat . . .

Somehow,
I couldn't get past
that prison train
that kept waking me up
every night.
I couldn't get that whistle
that rumble
out of my head . . .

In this classroom
austerely furnished
by my insomnia,
at the desk consisting
of my two knees,
for the first time
in this long and terrifying
apprenticeship,
I burst out laughing.
Forgive me, all of you!
At the memory of my uncle
charging a barricade
with a homemade bomb,
I burst out laughing.

A Landscape with Crutches

So many crutches. Now even the daylight
Needs one, even the smoke
As it goes up. And the shacks—
One per customer—they move off
In a single file with difficulty,

I said, with a hell of an effort . . .
And the trees behind them about to stumble,
And the ants on their toy crutches,
And the wind on its ghost crutch.

I can't get any peace around here:
The bread on its artificial limbs,
A headless doll in a wheelchair,
And my mother, mind you, using
Two knives for crutches as she squats to pee.

The Variant

A police dog eating grass
On a coroner's leash
Along the perimeter
Of barbed wire.

His impeccable table manners
And the evening's capacity
For lofty detachment
From the extraordinary event.

The grass like a prophet's beard,
Thoughtful and graying. Chill
Of late autumn in the air.
Distant guard towers with searchlights
Following us all
With malice, regret,
And also absentmindedly.

The proverbial dry blades
Sticking in the throat.

Obviously, what the poor mutt needs
Is a mean old stepmother
To tap him on the back
Quickly
Not caring to hold on.

The Summons

The robes of the judges are red
As they take their high seats.
The one with the head of a lamb will be mine,
With a throat of a lamb newly slit.

The one splattered with mud,
Who rests his cheek against my writ,
Who has straw sticking out of his ear,
Who presides in this old courtroom.

This huge ruin with its roof gone,
So we can see the sky. A few snowflakes
Whirling in the vast empty space
Over which we address one another,

Over which we proclaim our innocence,
These snowflakes as our witnesses,
And the old women who sweep them
Knowing each flake by its suffering and its name.

Poem

My father writes all day, all night:
Writes while he sleeps, writes in his coffin.
It's nice and quiet in our house.
You can see the specks of dust in the sunlight.

I look at times over his shoulders
At all that whiteness. The snow is falling,
As you'd expect. A drop of ink
Gets buried easily, like a footprint.

I, too, would get lost but there's his shadow
On the wall, like a perched owl.
There's the sound of his pen
And the bottle on the table sunk in thought.

When the bottle empties
His great dark hand
Bigger than the earth
Feels for the moon's spigot.

Nursery Rhyme

The little pig goes to market.
Historical necessity. I like to recite
While you prefer to write on the blackboard.
Leap frogs and marbles.

Their heads are big and their noses are short.
Lovely afternoon. The firing squad.
A street maimed so it can go on begging.
Eternal recurrence and its trash heap.

Follow your calling, we follow ours.
The soldier's hand is gentle. The green meadow.
People who snore have happy dreams.
Our father in heaven loves us all.

A pig with gold teeth, says the barber.
Banks of a river lined with willows.
Now someone's kicking him to hurry up.
Rope, give a drink of milk to the rope.

I need another cigarette quickly.
An execution. The old wedding photograph.
I see a blur, a speck, meager, receding,
Our lives trailing in its wake.

Help Wanted

They ask for a knife
I come running
They need a lamb
I introduce myself as the lamb

A thousand sincere apologies
It seems they require some rat poison
They require a shepherd
For their flock of black widows

Luckily I've brought my bloody
Letters of recommendation
I've brought my death certificate
Signed and notarized

But they've changed their minds again
Now they want a songbird, a bit of springtime
They want a woman
To soap and kiss their balls

It's one of my many talents
(I assure them)
Chirping and whistling like an aviary
Spreading the cheeks of my ass

Animal Acts

A bear who eats with a silver spoon.
Two apes adept at grave digging.
Rats who do calculus.
A police dog who copulates with a woman,
Who takes undertaker's measurements.

A bedbug who suffers, who has doubts
About his existence. The miraculous
Laughing dove. A thousand-year-old turtle
Playing billiards. A chicken who
Cuts his own throat, who bleeds.

The trainer with his sugar cubes,
With his chair and whip. The evenings
When they all huddle in a cage,
Smoking cheap cigars, lazily
Marking the cards in the new deck.

Charon's Cosmology

With only his dim lantern
To tell him where he is
And every time a mountain
Of fresh corpses to load up

Take them to the other side
Where there are plenty more
I'd say by now he must be confused
As to which side is which

I'd say it doesn't matter
No one complains he's got
Their pockets to go through
In one a crust of bread in another a sausage

Once in a long while a mirror
Or a book which he throws
Overboard into the dark river
Swift and cold and deep

Happy End

And then they pressed the melon
And heard it crack
And then they ate enough to burst
And then the bird sang oh so sweetly
While they sat scratching without malice
Good I said for just then
The cripples started dancing on the table
That night I met a kind of angel
Do you have a match she said
As I was unzipping her dress
Already there were plenty of them
Who had ascended to the ceiling
Lovers they were called and they held
Roses between their teeth while the Spring
Went on outside the wide open windows
And even a stick used in child beating
Blossomed by the little crooked road
My hunch told me to follow

The Ballad of the Wheel

so that's what it's like to be a wheel
so that's what it's like to be tied to one of its spokes
while the rim screeches while the hub grinds
so that's what it's like to have the earth and heaven
    confused
to speak of the stars on the road
of stones churning in the icy sky
to suffer as the wheel suffers
to bear its unimaginable weight

if only it were a honing wheel
I would have its sparks to see by
if only it were a millstone
I would have bread to keep my mouth busy
if only it were a roulette wheel
my left eye would watch its right dance in it

so that's what it's like
to be chained to the wounded rib of a wheel
to move as the hearse moves
to move as the lumber truck moves
down the mountains at night

*

what do you think my love
while the wheel turns

I think of the horse out in front
how the snowflakes are caught in his mane
how he shakes his beautiful blindfolded head
I think how in the springtime
two birds are pulling us along as they fly
how one bird is a crow

and the other a swallow
I think how in the summertime
there's no one out there
except the clouds in the blue sky
except the dusk in the blue sky
I think how in autumn
there's a man harnessed out there
a bearded man with the bit stuck in his mouth
a hunchback with a blanket over his shoulders
hauling the wheel
heavy as the earth

*

don't you hear I say don't you hear
the wheel talks as it turns

I have the impression that it's hugging me closer
that it has maternal instincts
that it's telling me a bedtime story
that it knows the way home
that I grit my teeth just like my father

I have the impression
that it whispers to me
how all I have to do
to stop its turning
is to hold my breath

A Wall

That's the only image
That turns up.

A wall all by itself,
Poorly lit, beckoning,
But no sense of the room,
Not even a hint
Of why it is I remember
So little and so clearly:

The fly I was watching,
The details of its wings
Glowing like turquoise.
Its feet, to my amusement
Following a minute crack—
An eternity
Around that simple event.

And nothing else; and nowhere
To go back to;
And no one else
As far as I know to verify.

The Guest

Would he be the one
Awake in a strange room
After a long nap,

The one trying to remember
How he got there,
What he did
Before he went to bed,

Asking himself
Was a raindrop of the windowpane,
A footstep close by,

Or was it silence
That made him wake
Cold and so afraid?

     *

No one at all.

A bed to stretch out on,
Make one inconspicuous,
Exist
On the verge of disappearance,

A lone shadow puppet
Sagging on the mute
Whitewashed wall.

Voices of children
In the street.
Half-muffled games
Of some other century.

Purple clouds,
Slowly darkening clouds,
Like stooped widows
On their way
To light the lamps
At the far ends of the earth.

Description

That which brings it
about. The cause.

The sweet old temptation
to find an equivalent

for the ineffable:
This street, this gray day

breaking. So many things
for which to find a name.

Standing here, partaking
of that necessity.

*

Among all the sights
that offer themselves,

where to begin?
The visible, the invisible—

the many shapes pain assumes?
This old woman, for instance,

with a lame child,
leading her by the hand,

the way they suffer
to take every little step.

                *

A street that always
somehow resembles me.

Gray day and I
the source of its grayness.

A corner where
a part of myself

keeps an appointment
with another part of myself.

This small world.
This dumb show.

                *

The two of them
all hunched up,

hand in hand,
afraid to cross the street

on some age-old errand
to a store, a hospital

where the grim doctor
won't use any anesthetic

when he takes bread
out of their mouths.

The Terms

of what?
of life?

A child crying in the night
Across the street
In one of the many/dark windows.
That, too, to get used to,
Make part of your life.
Like this book of astronomy
Which you open with equal apprehension
By the light of table lamp,
And your birdlike shadow on the wall.
A sleepless witness at the base
Of this expanding immensity,
Simultaneous in this moment
With all of its empty spaces,
Listening to a child crying in the night
With a hope,
It will go on crying a little longer.

The opposition of one child and the many dark windows ... one imagines more children

The many dark windows as, in a sense space

opposition of light and dark, both net of apprehension

equal to what?

The apprehension of making the crying child a part of your life—

universe

The empty spaces of any moment

"Sleepless witness" a very strange phrase, something to expect! The body, even asleep, bears witness to the immensity of the universe

The single stanza form is mimetic of a list, a list of terms

This is a dark and eery ending, because if the crying continues the child is alive?

124.

Eraser

A summons because the marvelous prey is fleeing
Something to rub out the woods
From the blackboard sound of wind and rain
A device to recover a state of pure expectancy

Only the rubbings only the endless patience
As the clearing appears the clearing that is there
Without my even having to look
The domain of the marvelous prey

This emptiness that gets larger and larger
As the eraser works and wears out
As my mother shakes her apron full of little erasers
For me to peck like bread crumbs

*punctuation has been
erased*

Traveling Slaughterhouse

Dürer, I like that horse of yours.
I spent my childhood hidden in his guts.
The knight looks like my father
The day he came out of prison.

Maria, the redheaded girl goes by
Without giving us a nod. The knight says,
I get up at night to see if the table is still a table.
He says, when I close my eyes everything is so
    damn pretty.

We are dawdling in our old back alley.
I see a dog, a goat, but no death.
It must be one of those bleak breezy days in late
    autumn.
The horse uses his tail to hold up his pants.

Maria naked in front of a mirror eating an apple.
He says, I love the hair on the nipple to be blonde.
He says, we are a traveling slaughterhouse.
Ah the poor horse, he lets me eat his heart out!

Eyes Fastened with Pins

How much death works,
No one knows what a long
Day he puts in. The little
Wife always alone
Ironing death's laundry.
The beautiful daughters
Setting death's supper table.
The neighbors playing
Pinochle in the backyard
Or just sitting on the steps
Drinking beer. Death,
Meanwhile, in a strange
Part of town looking for
Someone with a bad cough,
But the address is somehow wrong,
Even death can't figure it out
Among all the locked doors . . .
And the rain beginning to fall.
Long windy night ahead.
Death with not even a newspaper
To cover his head, not even
A dime to call the one pining away,
Undressing slowly, sleepily,
And stretching naked
On death's side of the bed.

Trees at Night

Putting out the light
To hear them better.

*

To tell the leaves
Of an ash tree
Apart from those
Of a white birch.

*

They would both
Come closer,
They would both whisk me away.

*

Images of birds
Fleeing from a fire,
Images of a lifeboat
Caught in the storm.

*

The sound of those
Who sleep without dreams.

*

Being taken hold of
By them.
Being actively taken hold of,
Being carried off
In throes.

*

At times also like the tap
Of a moth
On a window screen.

*

A flurry of thoughts.
Sediments
On the bottom of night's ink,
Seething, subsiding.

*

Branches bending
To the boundaries
Of the inaudible.

*

A prolonged hush
That reminds me
To lock the doors.

*

Clarity.
The mast of my spine, for instance,
To which death attaches
A fluttering handkerchief.

*

And the wind makes
A big deal out of it.

Euclid Avenue

All my dark thoughts
laid out
in a straight line.

An abstract street
on which an equally abstract intelligence
forever advances, doubting
the sound of its own footsteps.

   *

Interminable cortege.
Language
as old as rain.
Fortune-teller's spiel

from where it has its beginning,
its kennel and bone,
the scent of a stick
I used to retrieve.

   *

A sort of darkness without the woods,
crow light but without the crow,

Hotel Splendide
all locked up for the night.

And out there,
in sight of some ultimate bakery
the streetlight
of my insomnia.

    *

A place
known as infinity
toward which that old self
advances.

The poor son of poor parents
who aspires to please
at such a late hour.

The magical coins
in his pocket
occupying all his thoughts.

A place known
as infinity,
its screen door screeching,
endlessly screeching.

The Prisoner

(He is thinking of us.)
These leaves, their lazy rustle
That made us sleepy after lunch
So we had to lie down.

He considers my hand on her breast,
Her closed eyelids, her moist lips
Against my forehead, and the shadows of trees
Hovering on the ceiling.

It's been so long. He has trouble
Deciding what else is there.
And all along the suspicion
That we do not exist.

[handwritten marginalia: "The first line is enclosed, like the prisoner / the second line enjambed, free, like the leaves, like the "we"" / "line break but hastens me, though the thought is full"]

A Day Marked with
a Small White Stone

The kindest of traps
Despite its immaculate steel,
And its powerful spring.
The bait, too, which one inhales
As if it were a scent of mint
The breeze is carrying.

The languorous, lazy chewing
On the caught leg
Gnawed down to the bone.
Pain joining the silence
Of trees and white clouds,

In a ring
Of magnanimous coyotes,
In a ring of
Dreamy, once-in-a-lifetime
Something or other.

Position without
a Magnitude

As when someone
You haven't noticed before
Gets up in an empty theater
And projects his shadow
Among the fabulous horsemen
On the screen

And you shudder
As you realize it's only you
On your way
To the blinding sunlight
Of the street.

Untitled

Aunt Lettuce, I want to peek under your skirt.

Primer

This kid got so dirty
Playing in the ashes

When they called him home,
When they yelled his name over the ashes,

It was a lump of ashes
That answered.

Little lump of ashes, they said,
Here's another lump of ashes for dinner,

To make you sleepy,
And make you grow strong.

School for Dark Thoughts

At daybreak,
Little one,
I can feel the immense weight
Of the books you carry.

Anonymous one,
I can hardly make you out
In that large crowd
On the frozen playground.

Simple one,
There are rulers and sponges
Along the whitewashed walls
Of the empty classroom.

There are windows
And blackboards,
One can only see through
With eyes closed.

Empire of Dreams

On the first page of my dreambook
It's always evening
In an occupied country.
Hour before the curfew.
A small provincial city.
The houses all dark.
The storefronts gutted.

I am on a street corner
Where I shouldn't be.
Alone and coatless
I have gone out to look
For a black dog who answers to my whistle.
I have a kind of Halloween mask
Which I am afraid to put on.

Prodigy

I grew up bent over
a chessboard.

I loved the word *endgame.*

All my cousins looked worried.

It was a small house
near a Roman graveyard.
Planes and tanks
shook its windowpanes.

A retired professor of astronomy
taught me how to play.

That must have been in 1944.

In the set we were using,
the paint had almost chipped off
the black pieces.

The white King was missing
and had to be substituted for.

I'm told but do not believe
that that summer I witnessed
men hung from telephone poles.

I remember my mother
blindfolding me a lot.
She had a way of tucking my head
suddenly under her overcoat.

In chess, too, the professor told me,
the masters play blindfolded,
the great ones on several boards
at the same time.

Baby Pictures of Famous Dictators

The epoch of a streetcar drawn by horses,
The organ-grinder and his monkey.
Women with parasols. Little kids in rowboats
Photographed against a cardboard backdrop depicting
    an idyllic sunset
At the fairgrounds where they all went to see
The two-headed calf, the bearded
Fat lady who dances the dance of seven veils.

And the great famine raging through India . . .
Fortune-telling white rat pulling a card out of a shoebox
While Edison worries over the lightbulb,
And the first model of the sewing machine
Is delivered in a pushcart
To a modest white-fenced home in the suburbs,

Where there are always a couple of infants
Posing for the camera in their sailors' suits,
Out there in the garden overgrown with shrubs.
Lovable little mugs smiling faintly toward
The new century. Innocent. Why not?
All of them like ragdolls of the period
With those chubby porcelain heads
That shut their long eyelashes as you lay them down.

In a kind of perpetual summer twilight . . .
One can even make out the shadow of the tripod and
    the black hood
That must have been quivering in the breeze.
One assumes that they all stayed up late squinting at
    the stars,
And were carried off to bed by their mothers and
    big sisters,
While the dogs remained behind:
Pedigreed bitches pregnant with bloodhounds.

Whispers

The hospital barber next door,
Who shaves stroke victims,
Shaves the dying.
Shaves the mad chained to their beds,

Is a shuffling old widower,
Has a line of ants waiting at home,
A can of baked beans
He eats cold with a coffee spoon,

Says: where did all the years go by,
O Lord, bent as I was intently
Over the razor, my hand shaking
Once in a long while.

Shirt

To get into it
As it lies
Crumpled on the floor
Without disturbing a single crease

Respectful
Of the way I threw it down
Last night
The way it happened to land

Almost managing
The impossible contortions
Doubling back now
Through a knotted sleeve

Great Infirmities

Everyone has only one leg.
So difficult to get around,
So difficult to climb the stairs
Without a cane or a crutch to our name.

And only one arm. Impossible contortions
Just to embrace the one you love,
To cut the bread on the table,
To put a coat on in a hurry.

I should mention that we are almost blind,
And a little deaf in both ears.
Perilous to be on the street
Among the congregations of the afflicted.

With only a few steps committed to memory,
Meekly we let ourselves be diverted
In the endless twilight—
Blind seeing-eye dogs on our leashes.

An immense stillness everywhere
With the trees always bare,
The raindrops coming down only halfway,
Coming so close and giving up.

The Healer

In a rundown tenement
Under the superhighway,
A healer lives
Who doesn't believe in his power.

An old man with a fat gut,
Hands of a little girl
Which he manicures himself,
Carefully, between visits.

In his hallway there are
Many wheelchairs, on the stairs
The long howl of the idiot
Led on his mother's leash.

Navigator

I thought of Christopher Columbus.
At four in the morning,
He stepped out of the shadows
Looking like my dead father.

On this long voyage
He found no sign of land,
Only the boundless
In its awful majesty.

His old sailing ship was an eye
That watched the eye
That watched the eye.
His ears were the sails.

At first, there were stars,
And then not even that.
Just night everywhere
And the open sea

With a deep calm over it,
That was there
Long before there were words,
And long after them.

A Suitcase Strapped with a Rope

for Jim

They made themselves so tiny
They could all fit in one suitcase.
The suitcase they kept under the bed,
And the bed near the open window.

They huddled there in the dark
While their mother called out their names
To make sure no one was missing.
Her voice made them warm, made them sleepy.

He wanted to go out and play.
He even asked for permission.
They told him to be very quiet.
Just then the suitcase was moving.

Soon the border guards were going
To open it and inspect it,
Unless, of course, it was a burglar
And he knew another way to go.

Begotten of the Spleen

The Virgin Mother walked barefoot
Among the land mines.
She carried an old man in her arms
Like a howling babe.

The earth was an old people's home.
Judas was the night nurse,
Emptying bedpans into the river Jordan,
Tying people on a dog chain.

The old man had two stumps for legs.
St. Peter came pushing a cart
Loaded with flying carpets.
They were not flying carpets.

They were piles of bloody diapers.
The Magi stood around
Cleaning their nails with bayonets.
The old man gave little Mary Magdalene

A broken piece of a mirror.
She hid in the church outhouse.
When she got thirsty she licked
The steam off the glass.

That leaves Joseph. Poor Joseph,
Standing naked in the snow.
He only had a rat
To load his suitcases on.

The rat wouldn't run into its hole.
Even when the lights came on—
And the lights came on:
The floodlights in the guard towers.

Toy Factory

My mother works here,
And so does my father.

It's the night shift.
At the assembly line,
They wind toys up
To inspect their springs.

The seven toy members
Of the firing squad
Point their rifles,
And lower them quickly.

The one being shot at
Falls and gets up,
Falls and gets up.
His blindfold is just painted on.

The toy gravediggers
Don't work so well.
Their spades are heavy,
Their spades are much too heavy.

Perhaps that's how
It's supposed to be?

The Little Tear Gland That Says

Then there was Johann,
the carousel horse—
except he wasn't really a carousel horse.

He grew up in "the naive realism of the Wolffian school
which without close scrutiny regards
logical necessity and reality as identical."

On Sundays, his parents took him
to the undertaker's for sugar.
"All these people flying in their dreams,"
he thought.

Standing before the Great Dark Night of History,
a picture of innocence
held together by his mother's safety pins,
frisky, wagging his tail.

Cool reflection soon showed
there were openings among the signatories of death
    certificates . . .
with those high leather boots that squeak.

On his entrance exam he wrote:
"The act of torture consists of various strategies
meant to increase the imagination
of the *Homo sapiens.*"

And then . . . the Viennese waltz.

The Stream

for Russ Banks

The ear threading
the eye

all night long
the ear
on a long errand
for the eye

through the thickening
pine
white birch
over no-man's-land

pebbles
is it
compact in their anonymity
their gravity

accidents of location
abstract necessity

water
which takes such pains

to convince me
it is flowing

*

Summoning me
to be
two places at once

to drift
the length
of its chill
its ache

hand white
at the knuckles

live bait
the old hide-and-seek
in and out
of the swirl

luminous verb
carnivorous verb
innocent as sand
under its blows

*

An insomnia as big
as the stars'

always
on the brink—
as it were
of some deeper utterance

some harsher
reckoning

at daybreak
lightly
oh so lightly
when she brushes
against me

and the hems of her long skirt
go trailing

a bit longer

*

Nothing
that comes to nothing
for company

comes the way a hurt
the way a thought
comes

comes and keeps coming

all night meditating
on what she asks of me
when she doesn't

when I hear myself say
she doesn't

Immortal Prankster

When a cuckoo comes to the village
Of cuckoos to cuckoo and it's Monday,
And all the cuckoos should be there cuckooing,
But instead there's no one at home

Nor inside the little red schoolhouse,
Or even in the great old trees lining the road,
Well then, the cuckoo who came to the village
Of cuckoos to cuckoo must cuckoo all alone.

Furniture Mover

Ah the great
   the venerable
whoever he is

   ahead of me
huge load
   terrific backache

   wherever
a chair's waiting
   meadow
sky
   beckoning

he is the one
   that's been
there
   without instructions
and for no wages

   a huge load
on his back
   and under his arm
thus
   always

all in place
perfect
just as it was
sweet home

at the address
I never even dreamed of
the address
I'm already changing

in a hurry
to overtake him
to arrive
not ahead

but just as
he sets down
the table
the thousand-year-old
bread crumbs

I used to
claim
I was part
of his load

high up there
roped safely

with the junk
the eviction notices

I used to
prophesy
he'll stumble
by and by

No luck—
oh
Mr. Furniture Mover
on my knees

let me come
for once
early
to where it's vacant

you still
on the stairs
wheezing
between floors

and me behind the door
in the gloom
I think I would
let you do

what you must

Elegy

Note
as it gets darker
　　that little
can be ascertained
of the particulars
　　and of their true
magnitudes

　　note
the increasing
　　unreliability
of vision
though one thing may appear
　　more or less
familiar
　　than another

　　disengaged
from reference
as they are
　　in the deepening
gloom

    nothing to do
but sit
    and abide
depending on memory
to provide
    the vague outline
the theory
of where we are
tonight

    and why
we can see
so little
    of each other
and soon
    will be
even less
    able

    in this starless
summer night
    windy and cold

    at the table
brought out
    hours ago
under a huge ash tree

two chairs
two ambiguous figures
    each one relying
on the other
to remain faithful
    now
that one can leave
    without the other one
    knowing

    this late
in what only recently was
    a garden
a festive occasion
    elaborately planned
for two lovers

    in the open air
at the end
    of a dead-end
road
    rarely traveled

    o love

Note Slipped under a Door

I saw a high window struck blind
By the late afternoon sunlight.

I saw a towel
With many dark fingerprints
Hanging in the kitchen.

I saw an old apple tree,
A shawl of wind over its shoulders,
Inch its lonely way
Toward the barren hills.

I saw an unmade bed
And felt the cold of its sheets.

I saw a fly soaked in pitch
Of the coming night
Watching me because it couldn't get out.

I saw stones that had come
From a great purple distance
Huddle around the front door.

December Trees

Bare woods, you made a tight circle
Around me as if making
A careful estimate from on high
On a matter known only to you.

For such is the season. Obligingly,
I stood like a horse about to be shod
In an old-time blacksmith's shop,
Smoke and steam nearly blinding me,

As your trees put on the aprons
Of approaching dusk and reached
Among the branches for the irons,
The ones with the sun setting on them.

Grocery

Figure or figures unknown
Keep a store
Keep it open
Nights and all day Sunday

Half of what they sell
Will kill you
The other half
Makes you go back for more

Too cheap to turn on the lights
Hard to tell what it is
They've got on the counter
What it is you're paying for

All the rigors
All the solemnities
Of a brass scale imperceptibly quivering
In the early winter dusk

One of its pans
For their innards
The other one for yours—
And yours heavier

Classic Ballroom Dances

Grandmothers who wring the necks
Of chickens; old nuns
With names like Theresa, Marianne,
Who pull schoolboys by the ear;

The intricate steps of pickpockets
Working the crowd of the curious
At the scene of an accident; the slow shuffle
Of the evangelist with a sandwich board;

The hesitation of the early-morning customer
Peeking through the window grille
Of a pawnshop; the weave of a little kid
Who is walking to school with eyes closed;

And the ancient lovers, cheek to cheek,
On the dance floor of the Union Hall,
Where they also hold charity raffles
On rainy Monday nights of an eternal November.

Progress Report

And how are the rats doing in the maze?
The gray one in a baggy fur coat
Appears dazed, the rest squeeze past him
Biting and squealing.

A pretty young attendant has him by the tail.
She is going to slit him open.
The blade glints and so do the beads
Of perspiration on her forehead.

His cousins are still running in circles.
The damp, foul-smelling sewer
Where they nuzzled their mother's teat
Is what they hope to see at the next turn.

Already she's yanked his heart out,
And he doesn't know what for?
Neither does she at this moment
Watching his eyes glaze, his whiskers twitch.

Harsh Climate

The brain itself in its skull
Is very cold,
According to
Albertus Magnus.

Something like a stretch of tundra
On the scale of the universe.
Galactic wind.
Lofty icebergs in the distance.

Polar night.
A large ocean liner caught in the ice.
A few lights still burning on the deck.
Silence and fierce cold.

Peaceful Kingdom

The bird who watches me
sleeping
from the branch of an apple tree
in bloom.

A blackbird
for whom a strange man
gathers rocks
in the ruts of the road.

    *

And among the willow trees:
water
before water made up its mind
to be water.

My sister says if I drink
of that water I will die . . .
That's why the heart beats:
to waken the water.

Bedtime Story

When a tree falls in a forest
And there's no one around
To hear the sound, the poor owls
Have to do all the thinking.

They think so hard they fall off
Their perch and are eaten by ants,
Who, as you already know, all look like
Little Black Riding Hoods.

The Tomb of
Stéphane Mallarmé

Beginning to know
   how the die
navigates
   how it makes
its fateful decisions
   in eternal circumstances
what it feels like
   to be held tight
between the thumb
   and the forefinger
to be hexed
   and prayed over
to wake up lucid
   at the heart of the shipwreck
a dark pilot's cabin
   of the die on the move
to have the earth and heaven
   repeatedly reversed
to have the mirror and the razor
   momentarily aligned
only to fall
   head over heels
to be set adrift
   in the middle of

nowhere
   the die
worn clean
   by endless conjectures
my die
   perfectly illegible
white
   as a milk tooth
the perfect die
   rolling
picking up speed
   how delightful
this new contingency
   occupancy
both inside and outside
   the unthinkable

the blindman's die
   free of
the divinatory urge
   the Number
even if it existed
   the death-defying
somersault
   beating the supreme odds
two by two
   along for the ride
only

        the roller coaster
endlessly changing directions
        and mind
in a state of blessed
        uncertainty
cast
        on the great improbable
table
        among the ghostly saltcellars
bones
        bread crumbs that say
there goes:
        Cerberus's new toy
Death's great amateur
        night
the childhood of Parmenides

oh yeah

Forest Birds

It! It!
That's what the unknown bird said,

and another answered,
in the same manner,

without identifying the agent:
some animal or thing.

Very cautious of them,
to be sure.

With the woods so thick and murky,
poor unknown . . .

A frailest twig,
and then the tip of that twig
to speak from . . .

It looks like it,
and it acts like it,
but who's to say?

*

That *it*
  has wish
that *it*
  has a wishbone

deep, deep
in all our throats

which is why the birds
are screeching . . .

in the vicinity of,
in the terrifying

nearness of . . .

 *

The woods of the obscure,
the hidden.

The woods of the lost,
the woods of the innermost,
inwrought, indwelling

object of our desire.

A name called from
one of its giddiest branches.

Odd name proclaimed
oddly.

Harken to *it* to be sure.

*

By eaves and leaves . . .

How like leave-
taking.

How like St. Francis
saying:

little brother
little sister.

Last half-note,
half-twig.

I'm very anxious,
they're very anxious

to have it remain
like that.

Figuring

A zero burped by
Another huger zero
That says woe woe!

The whole orphanage
Came out to see.

We gave it feathers,
Wings of an angel.
We gave it the shirt off our backs.

Potato head, egg of a snowy owl,
But the forest veiled,
The Papa and Mama forest.

Wintry pallor and ire.
Wind's rabies. Pitchy heavens.

Apes with rice-powdered asses.
Monday moving its dentures.

We give it a racehorse,
Windmills, an alarm clock with one hand.
Off it goes, trussed up, slaphappy.

At the other end of a zoo cage
A nurse waits for him,
Rainy days, stub of a pencil.

A zero. Write it kid!
And he writes it.
The dumb-looking one
At the blackboard.

History Book

A kid found its loose pages
On a busy street.
He stopped bouncing his ball
To run after them.

They fluttered in his hands
And flew off.
He could only glimpse
A few dates and a name.

At the outskirts the wind
Lost interest in them.
Some fell into the river
By the old railroad bridge

Where they drown kittens,
And the barge passes,
The one they named "Victory"
From which a cripple waves.

Black Days

Fellows, my teeth hurt,
And I've no money to have them pulled.
If you know a way, tell me.

The landlord knocked on my window.
My wife sleeps uncovered
So he just stood there staring,
Till he forgot what he came for.

The soles of my shoes have holes,
And the path to the mailbox is frozen.
If you know another way, tell me.

What else? I was born in wartime.
There was no money then either.

I licked the spoon every evening,
Then I licked the bowl carefully
While my mother sat and watched
Until she shuddered and hid her face.

Fool's Paradise

The word *lassitude*, for instance,
It goes well with bead curtains,
Bedroom eyes
And Turkish pillows on the floor.

Heavy-lidded demoiselle Isabelle
With a hookah and café au lait
At the fortune-teller's
With a bookie operating in the back.

Melancholia, her beautiful sister,
Is there too, like a smutty photo
A succubus dangles
Before a monk kneeling in prayer.

And as for me, Doc, the smoke
Rises among the paper lanterns
The black cat opens its pink mouth to yawn,
The babe is at its mother's breast.

Body and Soul

A soul hired a body
To be her handyman,
Fix what needs fixing
And make her say amen.

He fiddled with her radiator,
Diddled with her radio.
He even creamed her wheat
And threaded her needle.

The neighbors declared,
The fellow is a jailbird,
Has mermaids tattooed
Up and down his arms.

The once-proud soul pouted
Behind the curtains
Of softly falling rain
The color of bitten nails.

Venus

The well-lit,
All-night drugstore
In the sky
Open for business,

Something, please,
Miss.
To ease my fear
Of the dark.

She, not looking up,
Busy
Measuring
Into a vial

Drop after drop
Of that clear,
Odorless drug,
They call infinity.

Sewing Machine

The beast. Mourning cloth
Is what it eats
In the first light of day,
In the last light of day.

My mother bends over
As she serves
Handful after handful
Of what could be shadows.

A century of evenings,
Dark clouds advancing,
Stitch by bitter stitch
Across the bloody horizon.

Gravity

I'd like to see it once
As it lowers
Its fat foot
On our shoulders.

O Lord! That's what the choir
Of the Baptist church says,
And the trees agree
As they bend low in observance.

Sunday evening service
Where it wants the congregation
On its knees, sighing
And kissing the floor.

And later,
Still swaying under its weight,
Like beasts of burden,
Going home over the freshly fallen snow.

Northern Exposure

When old women say, it smells of snow,
In a whisper barely audible
Which still rouses the sick man upstairs
So he opens his eyes wide and lets them fill

With the grayness of the remaining daylight.
When old women say, how quiet it is,
And truly today no one came to visit,
While the one they still haven't shaved

Lifts the wristwatch to his ear and listens.
In it, something small, subterranean
And awful in intent, chews rapidly.
When old women say, time to turn on the lights,

And not a single one gets up to do so,
For now there are loops and loose knots around their feet
As if someone is scribbling over them
With a piece of charcoal found in the cold stove.

Winter Night

The church is an iceberg.

It's the wind. It must be blowing tonight
Out of those galactic orchards,
Their Copernican pits and stones.

The monster created by the mad Dr. Frankenstein
Sailed for the New World,
And ended up some place like New Hampshire.

Actually, it's just a local drunk,
Knocking with a snow shovel,
Wanting to go in and warm himself.

An iceberg, the book says, is a large drifting
Piece of ice, broken off a glacier.

The Cold

As if in a presence of an intelligence
Concentrating. I thought myself
Scrutinized and measured closely
By the sky and the earth,

And then algebraized and entered
In a notebook page blank and white,
Except for the faint blue lines
Which might have been bars,

For I kept walking and walking,
And it got darker and then there was
A flicker of a light or two
Far above and beyond my big cage.

A Fall Day

As gray as that slumped
Figure hands deep in his
Pockets receding on the
Gravelly road lean dogs
From the trailer park on
His ass the whole soulful
Lot of them fading away
Without *adieus* fading
Because of all the fine sands
Piling up on lunar deserts
Which have a way of sifting
Down this way the late
Autumn light already grainy
Gritty like poor eyesight
Gray bedsheets gray back
Of a woman combing her
Graying hair under the dead
Clock on the wall
Because truth's gray
Naked truth looking out
Vacant-eyed on the rain-
Blurred weedchoked outskirts
Of a dying mill town
Where her ancient mother

Keeps giving that last dime
To someone wearing a hood
Of yesterday's newspapers
Outside the urine-streaked
Theater lobby where on Saturday
Nights they've Live Wrestling
Teeth filed to razor's sharpness
Lion-roars mad-dog-bites
Backbreakers you'd hear in China
But now all of it mute cindery
Grim and earnest
Unlettered and benighted
I believe hieroglyphically

There They Stand Unaware
of Their Wretchedness

for Jim Tate

The philosopher Nietzsche
(Who said that),
Once supposedly shaved
A dray horse in Turin.

The same mad Nietzsche
Used to peek into his pocket mirror
From time to time,
To make sure he was still there.

I imagine, it must've been
The same mirror
He let the horse admire himself in
After the quick shave.

Further Adventures
of Charles Simic

Is our Charles Simic afraid of death?
Yes, Charles Simic is afraid of death.

Does he kneel and pray for eternal life?
No, he's busy drawing a valentine with a crayon.

Pale as a freshly chopped onion,
He goes over the wrongs he committed.

His conscience, does it bother him much?
Only when he lies down to get a night's rest.

The hellfires, does he feel them closing in?
No, but he hears the hounds barking.

Does he lift his eyes humbly in forgiveness?
Her love was his judge, her wrath the jury.

Some dark night, praying to the Lord above,
His own tongue will slash his throat.

Devotions

for Michael Anania

The hundred-year-old servants
Are polishing the family silver,
And recalling the little master dressed as a girl
Peeing in a chamber pot.

Now he is away hunting with Madame.
The reverend dropped by this afternoon
And inquired amiably after them.
His pink fingers were like squirming piglets.

Even the Siamese cats like to sit and gaze,
On days when it rains and the fire is lit,
At the grandfather with waxed mustache-tips
Scowling out of the heavy picture frame.

They were quick to learn respect
And what is expected of them, these former
Farm boys and girls stealing glances
At themselves in spoons large and small.

Shortcut

A real dark alley
That could take me
Home faster,
Full of men
With bloody hands.

Or far worse:
The lone sound of
My own footsteps,
Growing distant,
Or coming closer.

Old Couple

They're waiting to be murdered,
Or evicted. Soon
They expect to have nothing to eat.
In the meantime, they sit.

A violent pain is coming, they think.
It will start in the heart
And climb into the mouth.
They'll be carried off in stretchers, howling.

Tonight they watch the window
Without exchanging a word.
It has rained, and now it looks
Like it's going to snow a little.

I see him get up to lower the shades.
If their window stays dark,
I know his hand has reached hers
Just as she was about to turn on the lights.

Cold Blue Tinge

The pink-cheeked Jesus
Thumbtacked above
The cold gas stove,
And the boy sitting on the piss pot
Blowing soap bubbles
For the black kitten to catch.

Very peaceful, except
There's a faint moan
From the next room.
His mother's asking
For some more pills,
But there's no reply.
The bubbles are quiet,
And kitten is sleepy.

All his brothers and sisters
Have been drowned.
He'll have a long life, though,
Catching mice for the baker,
And the undertaker.

The Writings of the Mystics

On the counter among many
Much-used books,
The rare one you must own
Immediately, the one
That makes your heart race

As you wait for small change
With a silly grin
You'll take to the street,
And later, past the landlady
Watching you wipe your shoes,

Then, up to the rented room
Which neighbors the one
Of a nightclub waitress
Who's shaving her legs
With a door partly open,

While you turn to the first page
Which speaks of a presentiment
Of a higher existence
In things familiar and drab . . .

In a house soon to be torn down,
Suddenly hushed, and otherworldly . . .
You have to whisper your own name,
And the words of the hermit,

Since it must be long past dinner,
The one they ate quickly,
Happy that your small portion
Went to the three-legged dog.

Window Washer

one long sentence

And again the screech of the scaffold
High up there where all our thoughts converge:
Light-headed, hung
By a leather strap,

Twenty stories up
In the chill of late November
Wiping the grime
Off the pane, the many windows

Which have no way of opening,
Tinted windows mirroring the clouds
That are like equestrian statues,
Phantom liberators with sabers raised

Before these dark offices,
And their anonymous multitudes
Bent over this day's
Wondrously useless labor.

The Homeless

I saw many today
I will not forget.
They sat or lay down on the sidewalk,
As if kicked over.

Spilled rags
And old newspapers
All around them—
It was that chilly.

Faces covered up,
And only one eye
Drilling into me
With cold fury,

As if I were a long-legged
Tropical bird
Strutting over the snow
In his bright feathers.

Misfortune Is on the Way

And the day so mild
And cloudless.
The trees and the meadows
Are all in flower.

If there are children playing,
One of them is not.
He's looking your way.
Misfortune, riding

In your dark limousine,
Forget you ever saw him today.
Crows strutting in the road,
Mind your own business.

Keep your beaks shut,
Or at least warn him
With your caws and the sudden
Flapping of your wings.

Prison

That of the eyes
Opening in the morning
Upon the same
Old room:

With its chair,
Table, ceiling.
Solitary confinement
With a window,

View of treetops
Late-lingering moon
In the hush
The early hour.

The cat on the bed,
Who is the warden,
The purring messenger
Of my life sentence.

The Overcoat

Big enough for the two of us
To wear at the same time.
Tough to get around,
But we manage somehow

Our exit onto the street.
Mr. Policeman, we just require someone
To button it for us,
Stick a bouquet of roses

In one of the four hands
Jutting out of its sleeves.
We are off to a wedding,
And after that to a funeral.

The Game

A child played being a gravedigger.

Yellow pail and plastic shovel
On the green meadow.
Night coming.
Huge clouds rolling in.

With his stooped shoulders
He looks busy in the obvious way . . .
Dark, damp clods of earth flying.

They ought to call him in by now:
The carrot-haired girl in the henhouse;
Her sister at the salt lick.

Gallows Etiquette

Our sainted great-great
Grandmothers
Used to sit and knit
Under the gallows.

No one remembers what it was
They were knitting
And what happened when the ball of yarn
Rolled out of their laps
And had to be retrieved.

One pictures the hooded executioner
And his pasty-faced victim
Interrupting their grim business
To come quickly to their aid.

Confirmed pessimists
And other party poopers
Categorically reject
Such far-fetched notions
Of gallows etiquette.

In Midsummer Quiet

Ariadne's bird,
That lone
Whippoorwill.

Ball of twilight thread
Unraveling furtively.
Tawny thread,
Raw, pink the thread end.

A claw or two also
To pare, snip . . .
After which it sits still
For the stream to explain why it shivers

So.
      Resuming, farther on,
Intermittently,
By the barn
Where the first stars are—
In quotation marks,
As it were—O phantom

Bird!
Dreaming of my own puzzles
And mazes.

Peaceful Trees

in memory of M. N.

All shivers,
Dear friends.

Is it for me
You keep still?

Not a rustle
To remind me—

Quietly, the healing
Spreads—

A deep shade
Over each face.

    *

So many leaves,
And not one
Lately stirring.

So many already
Tongue-shaped,
Tip of the tongue shaped.

Oh the sweet speech of trees
In the evening breeze
Of some other summer.
Speech like sudden
Rustle of raindrops
Out of the high, pitch-blue
Heavens.

Lofty ones,
Do you shudder
When the chain saw
Cuts one of you?

Would it soothe,
If for all you voiceless,
To high heavens
The one with the rope round his neck

Were to plead?

*

Forgive me,

For the conjecture
I'm prone to—

Restless as I am
Before you windless,

Whispering
To the Master Whisperers

Of their own
Early evening silences.

The Unknown One

Some Power Company employee
Whose job it is
To switch on the streetlights
In my neighborhood.

It's almost night now,
And he hasn't done it yet,
Whoever he is, must have other things
Weighing on his mind,

For all we know,
Is roaming these same streets,
Hands in his pockets,
Bumping into us,

Sorry and all that . . .
Standing here on the corner,
Smoking butts and gabbing.
Stealing peeks at the stars too.

Chairs

More and more empty chairs.

I just lit a match
In broad daylight
To make sure.

Yes, empty chairs everywhere—

Except, where did
Everybody go?
I dared not ask aloud

With the match
Burning down to my fingers.

My Beloved

after D. Khrams

In the fine print of her face
Her eyes are two loopholes.
No, let me start again.
Her eyes are flies in milk,
Her eyes are baby Draculas.

To hell with her eyes.
Let me tell you about her mouth.
Her mouth's the red cottage
Where the wolf ate grandma.

Ah, forget about her mouth,
Let me talk about her breasts.
I get a peek at them now and then
And even that's more than enough
To make me lose my head,
So I better tell you about her legs.

When she crosses them on the sofa
It's like the jailer unwrapping a parcel
And in that parcel is a Christmas cake
And in that cake a sweet little file
That gasps her name as it files my chains.

Gospel Hour

Mary Magdalene lives over the grocery store.
She wears a Salvation Army uniform when she
    steps out to dump the trash.
Rats make way for her to the overflowing bin.
The Jesus look-alike has a pigeon coop on the roof.
If the doves are not cooing, he is.
One Saturday he knocks on her door. It's unlocked.
She's on the floor undressing a doll,
First the blue jacket with gold buttons comes off,
Then the short pants, and finally the white socks
Which she pulls and pulls with her teeth.

A Quiet Talk with Oneself

As spring flowers are promised by
Seed sellers in their new catalogues,
You too were once full of promise,
Only to lapse, woefully, my friend.

Cultivated garden's perfect rows
Marshaling their bright colors—
How I hate such images—
Some rosy-cheeked Rose clipping sweetheart roses

For the ass's wreath, the dull-eyed one who ought to
    be rapt,
What with his easy source of sustenance:
Pulling loads of potatoes, an occasional coffin,
Or just a cart full of happy children at the fair.

It seems to me these moods are best walked off
In a straight line toward some provisional infinity,
With many head shakes, groans too,
Under the leaves which must wonder at their own
    gradual disappearance.

But I digress. Just like that unfortunate Mr. Poe:
Compulsive ratiocination on the subject of the self

In the guise of a polar voyage without the means of
    retreat,
While the poor ass keeps getting whipped and rained on.

Each one of us like an ex-waiter, slightly bowed,
A linen napkin still in the crook of the arm,
Eyes on the lookout for some angelic customer to serve—
Some Daisy picking poppies instead of daisies.

Hurricane Season

Just as the world was ending
We fell in love,
Immoderately. I had a pair of

Blue pinstripe trousers
Impeccably pressed
Against misfortune;

You had a pair of silver,
Spiked-heeled shoes,
And a peekaboo blouse.

We looked swank kissing
While reflected in a pawnshop window:
Banjos and fiddles around us,

Even a gleaming tuba. I said,
Two phosphorescent minute hands
Against the Unmeasurables,

Geniuses when it came to
Undressing each other
By slow tantalizing degrees . . .

That happened in a crepuscular hotel
That had seen better days,
Across from some sort of august state institution,

Rain-blurred
With its couple of fake
Egyptian stone lions.

Note

A rat came on stage
During the performance
Of the school Christmas play.
Mary let out a scream
And dropped the infant
On Joseph's foot.
The three Magi remained
Frozen
In their colorful robes.
You could hear a pin drop
As the rat surveyed the manger
Momentarily
Before proceeding to the wings
Where someone hit him,
In earnest,
Once, and then twice more,
With a heavy object.

An Evening with the Master

With a stick and a leather glove,
He goads my soul
Out of its gilded cage,
Makes it sit in the palm of his hand,

Teaches it to trace with its beak,
As in a mirror,
The maze in my head:
Its scribblelike thoughts,
Its tangle of dead-ends.

A soul wearing a falcon's hood
As it bends over a school slate
Which lets out little squeaks
As it lets itself be written on.

Spoons with Realistic
Dead Flies on Them

I cause a great many worries to my mother.
My body will run with the weeds some day.
My head will be carried by slaughterhouse ants,
The carnivorous, bloody-aproned ants.

That was never in any of your legends, O saints!
The years she spent working in a novelty store:
Joy buzzers, false beards, and dead flies
To talk to between the infrequent customers.

A room rented from a minor demon.
An empty bird cage and a coffee mill for company.
A hand-operated one for her secret guardian angel
To take a turn grinding the slow hours.

Though I'm not a believer—
Neither is she, and that's why she worries,
Looks both ways crossing the street
At two gusts of nothing and nothing.

History

On a gray evening
Of a gray century,
I ate an apple
While no one was looking.

A small, sour apple
The color of wood fire
Which I first wiped
On my sleeve.

Then I stretched my legs
As far as they'd go,
Said to myself
Why not close my eyes now

Before the late
World News and Weather.

Rough Outline

The famous torturer takes a walk
Whom does he see standing there in the snow
A pretty girl in a wedding dress
What are you doing out there all alone in the cold

You're the famous torturer much feared
I beg you to spare my love
Who is in your darkest prison cell
I wish to marry him etc.

I will not give back your bridegroom
He must be tortured tonight
By me personally
You can come along and help him lament his fate

She remained where she was
The night was cold and very long
Down by the slaughterhouse a doglike creature howled
Then the snow started to fall again

Strictly Bucolic

for Mark and Jules

Are these mellifluous sheep,
And these the meadows made twice-melliferous by
    their bleating?
Is that the famous mechanical windup shepherd
Who comes with instructions and service manual?

This must be the regulation white fleece
Bleached and starched to perfection,
And we could be posing for our first communion
    pictures,
Except for the nasty horns.

I am beginning to think this might be
The Angelic Breeders Association's
Millennial Company Picnic (all expenses paid)
With a few large black dogs as special guests.

These dogs serve as ushers and usherettes.
They're always studying the rules,
The exigencies of proper deportment
When they're not reading Theocritus,

Or wagging their tails at the approach of
Theodora. Or is it Theodosius? Or even Theodoric?
They're theomorfic, of course. They theologize.
Theogony is their favorite. They also love theomachy.

Now they hand out the blue ribbons.
Ah, there's one for everyone!
Plus the cauldrons of stinking cabbage and boiled turnips
Which don't figure in this idyll.

Crows

Just so that each stark,
Spiked twig,
May be even more fierce
With significance,

There are these birds
As further harbingers
Of the coming wintry reduction
To sign and enigma:

The absolutely necessary
Way in which they shook snow
Out of their wings,
And then remained, inexplicably

Thus, wings half-open,
Making two large algebraic X's
As if for emphasis,
Or in the mockery of . . .

February

The one who lights the wood stove
Gets up in the dark.

How cold the iron is to the hand
Groping to open the flue,
The hand that will draw back
At the roar of the wind outside.

The wood that no longer smells of the woods;
The wood that smells of rats and mice—
And the matches that are always so loud
In the glacial stillness.

By its flare you'll see her squat;
Gaunt, wide-eyed;
Her lips saying the stark headlines
Going up in flames.

Inheritance

This is my father's gray blanket.
He used to lie under it anonymous:
Head and face hidden, bare feet
Sticking out, their toes clenched.

On a windy November afternoon,
The house cold, even
The bright sunlight chilling,
Just as it is now—

Like a steel tape measure
Estimating the anatomy of the sleeper,
The position of the heart
Under this blanket meant for a narrow bed—

An army cot perhaps? O recruits,
Prisoners! I believe one covers one's head
Because the lights are left on
In cells throughout the night.

The Amazing Potato Peeler

Right here in the street,
He's going to show us how it works,
On a card table not too steady
On this cold and windy night.

The cut-rate stores quickly closing,
A few rat-faced old women
Scurrying past without a glance,
And a lone hooker, in scarlet wig,
Rabbit fur coat, white boots,
Who rushes over interested.

Just for her, he's peeling a new one,
Himself in bad need of a shave.
No coat on his back, not even a hat—
And his head as bald as a potato.

A Tub

On four lions' paws
Into which a swan-necked
Copper faucet drips
Throughout the night.

The grave deliberations
Of phantom courts
And their hanging juries
Over the fate of each drop.

Lengthy pauses
In which to raise and cock
The blade
Of the guillotine,

Imagine the drop's
Convolutions,
The short, half-muffled
Cry of its name,

As it tumbles,
Head-first,
With a plunk
Into the drain.

Fable

for Mekeel

In my favorite one,
The fox is nagging
The bloody crow to sing.

He's perched in
A dead oak tree
Surveying acres of snow.

The winter evening,
Silent, starless
And evilly cold.

We know he shuts
His eyes tight
In a dreamy kind of way.

The fox is long gone
And so is the summer's
Hand-clapping thunder.

Ah, the future pop star
Croaking his first notes, blown away
By the beauty of his voice.

Punch Minus Judy

Where the elevated subway slows down,
A row of broken windows,
Only a single one still intact
Open and thickly curtained.

That's where I once saw a thin arm
Slip out between the slits,
The hand open to feel for drops of rain,
Or to give us a papal blessing.

Another time, there were two—
Chopped off at the elbows
Raising a small, naked baby
For a breath of evening air

Above the sweltering street
With a gang of men partying
Out of brown paper bags,
One limping off, seemingly, in a huff.

Small Wonders

The fellow no one ever looked at twice,
Comes to answer a marriage ad,
One drizzly November afternoon,
In a dining room full of old photos
And a cup of weak tea
With the bride's gray hair floating in it,
And her feverish story
Of how a handsome stranger once
Snatched her heart-shaped purse
On the way home from the evening Mass.

*

She saw the Angel of Death, too.
(That she told no one.)
In a back room of a notions store,
She sharpened the same pencil
With the same rusty razor blade.
Then she thought of her groom
Standing alone outside a movie house
His eyes red as if he had been
Chopping onions, but that can't be
Since that theater has been closed
For years, its screen a black hole.

*

Rosalia and her mother moved away,
But no one knows where and why.
At the baker's they pointed at the rolls
Lying rosy-cheeked in a pan like dolls.
In the church, there were postcards
Of the next life costing only a penny.
The undertaker knelt in front of me
To tie one black shoe. On the street,
Large snowflakes fell everywhere
Taking great care to mute every little sound.

Piety

A plain black cotton dress
On a wire hanger
In a closet otherwise empty,
Its door ajar to the light.

If you open your eyes,
You'll note it sways ever so slightly,
It shudders in the draft
Of undetermined origin.

Or is it your own breath?
Reaching that far
Despite the miles of frozen
Stubble, stone, earth.

If you close your eyes,
There's even a tiny rip
On the level of thighs,
The curlicue of blackest thread.

Austerities

From the heel
Of a half loaf
Of black bread,
They made a child's head.

Child, they said,
We've nothing for eyes,
Nothing to spare for ears
And nose.

Just a knife
To make a slit
Where your mouth
Ought to be.

You can grin,
You can eat,
Spit the crumbs
Into our faces.

Thus

Blue devils'
Bluest
Offspring—
My wife.

I said,
Pascal's own
Prize abyssologist
In marriage.

On her knees
Still scrubbing
The marble stairs
Of a Russian countess.

Once long ago in Paris
Gathering the butts
Outside the fashionable cafés
For her unemployed father.

Or in the New World
Naked before the grim
Doctor and nurse
A murmer in the heart.

Nevertheless, poking
The spit-moistened
End of a black thread
At the unblinking needle's eye,
Twelve hours a day.
A sublime seamstress,
An occupation hard on the backbone
And the eyesight.

On dark winter Sundays
Difficult to squint out
The letters and foreign words
In the night-school textbook.

All the carefully dog-eared,
Underlined passages
About lynchings, tar featherings,
Witch burnings—

Next to a cup of black coffee—
The kind storefront Gypsies make
When they sit staring at the rain,
Their lips just barely moving.

Shaving at Night

The profile of a man who waits
To be arrested at dawn.
If not this night, then
The next, the very next.

The small suitcases packed,
The wife and children long sent away,
He sits fully dressed
With the ashtray, the kitchen clock,

Thinking, maybe he should shave?
His face in the bathroom mirror
Lit by a dim bulb, one eye shut—
The face he won't look at closely—

Not yet anyway, while
There's still the upper lip to examine,
The trembling chin, the throat
With its large Adam's apple.

Eastern European Cooking

While Marquis de Sade had himself buggered—
O just around the time the Turks
Were roasting my ancestors on spits,
Goethe wrote "The Sorrows of Young Werther."

It was chilly, raw, down-in-the-mouth
We were slurping bean soup thick with smoked sausage,
On 2nd Avenue, where years before I saw an old horse
Pull a wagon piled up high with flophouse mattresses.

Anyway, as I was telling my uncle Boris,
With my mouth full of pig's feet and wine:
"While they were holding hands and sighing under
        parasols,
We were being hung by our tongues."

"I make no distinction between scum,"
He said, and he meant everybody,
Us and them: A breed of murderers' helpers,
Evil-smelling torturers' apprentices.

Which called for another bottle of Hungarian wine,
And some dumplings stuffed with prunes,
Which we devoured in silence
While the Turks went on beating their cymbals and drums.

Luckily we had this Transylvanian waiter,
A defrocked priest, ex-dancing school instructor,
Regarding whose excellence we were in complete
    agreement
Since he didn't forget the toothpicks with our bill.

The Childhood of Parmenides

for Elektra Haviaris

For asking, why is there something
Rather than nothing?
The schoolmaster sends the little punk
To see the Principal.

Unfortunately, they haven't got one yet.
There's only King Minos and his labyrinth,
And of course, Philemon, who's about to die laughing
At the sight of an ass eating figs.

Drawing the Triangle

I reserve the triangle
For the wee hours,
The chigger-sized hours.

I like how it starts out
And never gets there.
I like how it starts out.

In the meantime, the bedroom window
Reflecting the owlish aspect
Of the face and the interior.

One hopes for tangents
Surreptitiously in attendance
Despite the rigors of the absolute.

Interlude

A worm
In an otherwise
Red apple
Said: "I am."

It happened on a chipped
China plate,
At a table
With twelve empty chairs.

The rightful owner
Of the apple
Had gone into the kitchen
To get a knife.

She was an old woman
Who forgot things easily.
"Dear me,"
She whispered.

My Weariness
of Epic Proportions

I like it when
Achilles
Gets killed
And even his buddy Patroclus—
And that hothead Hector—
And the whole Greek and Trojan
Jeunesse dorée
Are more or less
Expertly slaughtered
So there's finally
Peace and quiet
(The gods having momentarily
Shut up)
One can hear
A bird sing
And a daughter ask her mother
Whether she can go to the well
And of course she can
By that lovely little path
That winds through
The olive orchard

Madonnas Touched Up with Goatees

Most ancient Metaphysics (poor Metaphysics!),
All decked out in imitation jewelry.
We went for a stroll, arm in arm, smooching in public
Despite the difference in ages.

It's still the 19th century, she whispered.
We were in a knife-fighting neighborhood
Among some rundown relics of the Industrial Revolution.
Just a little farther, she assured me,
In the back of a certain candy store only she knew about,
The customers were engrossed in the *Phenomenology of
the Spirit.*

It's long past midnight, my dove, my angel!
We'd better be careful, I thought.
There were young hoods on street corners
With crosses and iron studs on their leather jackets.
They all looked like they'd read Darwin and that
madman Pavlov,
And were about to ask us for a light.

Rural Delivery

I never thought we'd end up
Living this far north, love.
Cold blue heaven over our heads,
Quarter moon like chalk on a slate.

This week it's the art of subtraction
And further erasure that we study.
O the many blanks to ponder
Before the night overtakes us once more
On this lonely stretch of road
Unplowed since this morning;
Mittens raised against the sudden
Blinding gust of wind and snow,
But the mailbox empty. I had to stick
My bare hand all the way in
To make sure this is where we live.

The wonder of it! We retraced our steps
Homeward lit by the same fuel
As the snow glinting in the gloom
Of the early nightfall.

Old Mountain Road

for Goody and Maida Smith

In the dusk of the evening
When the goats come,
Two pale ones nodding as they pass,
Unattended, taking their time
To graze by the curve,
Its sharpness indicated by a broken arrow,
In the last bit of daylight,

I saw a blonde little girl step
Out of nowhere, and bow to them, stiffly,
As one does at the conclusion of a school play,
And disappear, pinafore and all,
In the bushes, so that I sat
On my porch, dumbfounded . . .

The goats' intermittent tinkle
Growing fainter and fainter,
And then hushing, as if on cue,
For the whippoorwill to take over,
Briefly, in the giant maple.

Child! I thought of calling out,
Knowing myself a born doubter.

The Great Horned Owl

One morning the Grand Seigneur
Is so good as to appear.
He sits in a scrawny little tree
In my backyard.

When I say his name aloud,
He turns his head
And looks at me
In utter disbelief.

I show him my belt,
How I had to
Tighten it lately
To the final hole.

He ruffles his feathers,
Studies the empty woodshed,
The old red Chevy on blocks.
Alas! He's got to be going.

Autumn Air

Many centuries ago in China
The sages debated the feasibility
Of dispelling hunger
By swallowing a lot of air,

In some godforsaken village,
There lived a poor man
Who kept striving all his life
To master the difficult art.
Finally, one lean day
He summoned his starving family.

His first steps, it seems,
Were scarcely elevated,
But then he rose confidently
Over the huts and the trees,
And the far-off royal palaces.

High in the sky, he drifted
Holding on to his straw hat
Among the razor-sharp,
Dragon-headed kites,
On his way out to sea,
The stormy, white-capped sea.

Midpoint

No sooner had I left A.
Than I started doubting its existence:
Its streets and noisy crowds;
Its famous all-night cafes and prisons.

It was dinnertime. The bakeries were closing:
Their shelves empty and white with flour.
The grocers were lowering their iron grilles.
A lovely young woman was buying the last casaba melon.

Even the back alley where I was born
Blurs, dims . . . O rooftops!
Armadas of bedsheets and shirts
In the blustery, crimson dusk . . .

    *

B. at which I am destined
To arrive by and by
Doesn't exist now. Hurriedly
They're building it for my arrival,

And on that day it will be ready:
Its streets and noisy crowds . . .
Even the schoolhouse where I first
Forged my father's signature . . .

Knowing that on the day
Of my departure
It will vanish forever
Just as A. did.

Drawn to Perspective

On a long block
Along which runs the wall
Of the House of Correction,
Someone has stopped
To holler the name
Of a son or a daughter.

Everything else in the world lies
As if in abeyance:
The warm summer evening;
The kid on roller skates;
The couple about to embrace
At the vanishing point.

The poems collected here were written between 1963 and 1983. Many first appeared in journals and magazines, often in different versions and under different titles. They were first published in book form in the following volumes:

What the Grass Says

    (Kayak, 1967)

        Butcher Shop

        Cockroach

        Evening

        Fear

        Marching

        Poem

        Summer Morning

        My Shoes

        Stone

Somewhere among Us a Stone Is Taking Notes

    (Kayak, 1969)

        Tapestry

        The Inner Man

Charon's Cosmology

(George Braziller, 1977)

Bedtime Story

The Tomb of Stéphane Mallarmé

Forest Birds

They Forage at Night

(Nadja, 1980)

Venus

Austerities

(George Braziller, 1982)

Hurricane Season

Note

An Evening with the Master

Spoons with Realistic Dead Flies on Them

History

Rough Outline

Strictly Bucolic

Crows

February

Inheritance

The Amazing Potato Peeler

A Tub

Fable

Punch Minus Judy

Small Wonders

Piety

Austerities

Weather Forecast for Utopia and Vicinity:
Poems, 1967–1982
   (Station Hill Press, 1983)

There They Stand Unaware
    of Their Wretchedness
Devotions
Shortcut
Old Couple
Cold Blue Tinge
The Writings of the Mystics
Window Washer
Prison
The Overcoat
The Game
Gallows Etiquette
In Midsummer Quiet
Peaceful Trees
The Unknown One
My Beloved
Gospel Hour
A Quiet Talk with Oneself

Pyramids and Sphinxes
    (Nadja, 1989)

    Fool's Paradise
    Misfortune Is on the Way
    Chairs